taking action

writing, reading, speaking, and listening through simulation-games

D1591462

LYNN QUITMAN TROYKA

JERROLD NUDELMAN

**Queensborough Community College
of the City University of New York**

PRENTICE-HALL, INC.
Englewood Cliffs, New Jersey

c. 9

Library of Congress Cataloging in Publication Data

TROYKA, LYNN QUITMAN, 1938
    Taking action

    Includes index.
    1. Language arts—Simulation methods.   2. English language—Study and
teaching—Simulation methods.   3. Simulation games in education.
I. Nudelman, Jerrold, 1942–   joint author.
II. Title.
LB1631.T76   420′.7   74-23252
ISBN   0-13-882571-8

PICTURE CREDITS

We would like to thank the following:

pp. 4, 5, 6–7, and 12–13, Cornell Capa (c) Magnum Photos, Inc.
pp. 8 and 9, drawings by George Remponeau.
pp. 10 and 57, (c) Leonard Freed—Magnum Photos, Inc.
p. 16, Shelley Katz—Black Star.
pp. 24–25, David Margolin—Black Star.
p. 27, courtesy of Chevrolet Motor Division, General Motors Corp.
p. 28, courtesy of Checker Motors Corporation.
p. 27, courtesy of Pratt Institute.
p. 38, John Collier—Black Star.
p. 41, EPA–DOCUMERICA—Doug Wilson.
p. 43, Burke Uzzle—Magnum Photos, Inc.
p. 52, THE NEW YORK TIMES/Michael Lien.
p. 55 and 60, (c) Police Foundation, Washington, D.C.,
    courtesy Catherine H. Milton.
p. 71, cartoon by Carol Reilly.
p. 72, top, courtesy of the Consulate General of the Netherlands.
p. 72, bottom, courtesy of Queensborough Community College.
p. 73, top, courtesy of Consolidated Edison of New York, Inc.
p. 73, center, (c) Segio Larrain—Magnum Photos, Inc.
p. 73, bottom, courtesy of Westinghouse Electric Corporation.
p. 82, Fritz Goro/Time–LIFE Picture Agency.
p. 84–5, Matt Franjola—Black Star.
pp. 88 and 89, courtesy of Dr. Landrum B. Shettles.
p. 92, I. A. Gonzalez—Black Star.

Printed in the United States of America

10 9 8 7 6 5 4 3 2

PRENTICE-HALL INTERNATIONAL, INC., *London*
PRENTICE-HALL OF AUSTRALIA, PTY. LTD., *Sydney*
PRENTICE-HALL OF CANADA, LTD., *Toronto*
PRENTICE-HALL OF INDIA PRIVATE LIMITED, *New Delhi*
PRENTICE-HALL OF JAPAN, INC., *Tokyo*

To our colleagues in the Basic Educational Skills
Department of Queensborough Community College,
for their enthusiastic professionalism and
their loyal friendship

and to David Troyka,
for his discerning criticisms and
unfailing moral support.

contents

SIMULATION-

GAMES

preface

The urge to communicate. We all have it. *Taking Action* harnesses the urge to communicate and structures it for the classroom through the technique of simulation-games.

Simulation-games originated years ago with the so-called "Pentagon war games." Like war games, simulation-games for the classroom are replications of a real environment that call for the participants to take action and make decisions as if they were actually operating in that environment. Social scientists have adapted simulation-games to the classroom to teach not only content such as political science and economics, but also the underlying human, social considerations that help shape decision making. Simulation-games were adapted for and used in the college English classroom when one of us, Lynn Quitman Troyka, did her doctoral dissertation on the subject. She wrote simulation-games for English, and, using experimental and control groups, measured the effect of the simulation-games on the students' expository prose competence. The results, explained in detail in the *Instructor's Guide* to *Taking Action*, were startlingly positive. The writing that resulted from the simulation-games demonstrated increased skill in reasoning, more clarity of writing style, and greater complexity of development.

Perhaps a key reason for this is that simulation-games provide students with a common ground of experience. No longer do students find themselves with "nothing to write about." For in simulation-games, situations are taken from real-life situations, structured roles correspond to those that are an integral part of the real situation, and supporting documentation replicates actual materials that pertain to the situation. The simulation-games in this book are designed for English instruction. Thus, they are more like highly structured experiental role-play than like complex simulations that rely on scoring, tokens, and so forth. What is important in this book is that the simulation-games by their very structure encourage communication: reading the simulation-game materials, speaking and listening within each simulation-game's context, and — as a direct, integrated follow-up — writing in response to the demands of each situation.

Taking Action contains six simulation-games, two taken from the original research mentioned above and four developed on the same theoretical and structural framework and then carefully classroom tested. The simulation-games in this book move from the less to the more intricate, but the progression is not at all lockstep. That is, the simulation-games can be played in whatever order is desired. The contexts of the simulation-games have to do with prison reform, car purchase, conservation, the roles of the sexes, government spending, and genetics and the family of the future. The simulation-game material includes photographs, graphs, cartoons, and drawings that encourage realistic visualization of the situation. The reality replication in each simulation-game is further supported by simulated documents that show students how real situations work. These include a prisoner orientation announcement, car sales brochures, chamber of commerce publications, a brief research study, a tourist brochure, and pages from a science manual.

The simulation-games in this book are easy to run. Each takes from thirty-five to fifty-five minutes, depending on the intricacy of the simulation-game and the pace set by the students and teacher. We have found that the more active the pace, the more involving the experience. Each simulation-game consists of four segments: role choice (five minutes), strategy round (seven to fifteen minutes), negotiation round (eighteen to twenty-five minutes), and decision making (five to ten minutes). These times are approximate and include students moving into and out of their group meeting (strategy round) and to the open meeting (negotiation round); it is the teacher who determines the actual time needed for each segment according to his or her impression of the students' needs. Aside from the teacher having to announce when the time for each segment is up, little supervision is necessary. Thus, the teacher can choose either to take a role or to circulate and coach.

Here's how to run a simulation-game: Each role is given to, or selected by, a different person, or if possible, group of persons. The idea is to involve as many people as possible; each simulation-game accommodates from five to thirty-six or more people. For ease of identification, each person writes his or her role-title on a name tag (blanks available page 143) and pins it on. Next, read the Situation Statement aloud, direct attention to the role descriptions and other game materials, and then have the members of each separate role-group meet to plan strategy: that is, what they will say at the upcoming open meeting. To help communication during the simulation-game, each person can use a "Simulation-Game Work Sheet." (One for each simulation-game is available at the back of the book.) After role-group planning, all roles come together into one group for negotiation at the open meeting: that is, the participants informally act out from their roles what they think would go on at such a meeting. Always, one role description in each game includes the direction to conduct the open meeting. Finally, the role-group responsible for making a decision confers and announces its ruling.

A simulation-game is over once the role-playing action has stopped. However, to continue the momentum from each simulation-game,

Taking Action includes, after the text of each simulation-game, an extensive list of "Communication Actions." These assignments, to be done in class or at home, as the teacher wishes, are not part of the simulation-games, but do relate to the general context of each situation and to related issues. Keyed to the four communication skills of writing, reading, speaking, and listening, the "Communication Actions" need not be done in order, nor is it expected that all will be done. Selections can be made according to interest and need for skill development.

To aid students working with the "Communication Actions," *Taking Action* includes at the end of the book a resource chapter on communication skills that presents basic principles and specific guidance for developing skill in writing, reading, speaking, and listening. The material is written for students who prefer direct, concise explanations that present essentials in a friendly, helpful format.

A special feature of *Taking Action* is the supplementary *Instructor's Guide* that offers advice on how to introduce simulation-games to the classroom, how to work with students during a simulation-game, and how to get the most from the text. Also included are additional "Communication Actions" for the six simulation-games, and an extensive list of related audio-visual materials, useful quotes by leading authorities on simulation-games, an annotated bibliography on simulation-games, ideas on conducting polls, and a detailed report on the research mentioned above.

Thus, *Taking Action: Writing, Reading, Speaking, and Listening Through Simulation-Games* has been designed with the view that from experience comes verbal fluency—and it is simulation-games that give students a chance to become immersed in lifelike, adult experiences that are both challenging and fun.

Lynn Quitman Troyka
Jerrold Nudelman

New York, 1975

acknowledgments

For their enormously useful comments on various parts of this book, we wish to thank: Judy Barbanel, Manette Reinitz Berlinger, Myra Kogen, Barbara Pennipede, Alvin Schlosser, Sandra Seltzer, and Meredith Young, all of Queensborough Community College. Also, for her friendship and very special artistic skills, we want to thank Carol Reilly, Spring Lake, New Jersey.

For their supportive, sensitive work with our manuscript at Prentice-Hall, we gratefully acknowledge: William Oliver, English Editor; Marilyn Brauer, Editor; Rita Kaye Schwartz, Designer; and Emily Dobson and Robb Reavill, Production Editors. Also, for their thorough, helpful reviews of our final manuscript, we sincerely thank: Marjorie Kroeger Blaha, San Jose City College, Paul Saylor, Northern Virginia Community College; and Patricia Williams, Bellevue Community College.

Finally, Lynn Quitman Troyka wishes to express her deep appreciation to her doctoral committee at New York University: Myron F. W. Pollack, Donald T. Payne, and John S. Mayher.

WHY SIMULATION-GAMES?

- Taking action—that's what many people dream of doing. The modern world is full of situations that cry out for action. Yet many people hesitate to get involved, and their dreams of what "could be" stay silently private and untried.

- Simulation-games give you the opportunity to experience the excitement and challenge of taking action in a complex world. That is, simulation-games give you a chance to take active, structured roles in simulated, lifelike situations that demand action and reaction.

- Simulation-games, just like life itself, tempt you to get involved. As you become involved, you'll find that communication skills such as speaking, listening, writing, and reading are a natural part of taking action.

SIMULATION-GAMES

uprising behind bars

*a simulation-game for English
about unrest in a state prison*

the roles

(5 to 35)

PRISONER

PRISON GUARD

WARDEN AND DEPUTY

CIVILIAN STAFF MEMBER

MEDIATOR

*uprising
behind
bars*

the situation

A serious crisis has developed at Medford Correctional Facility, a state prison for males in the United States. Until last week, inmate protests against the living conditions and rules in prison were constant, but mild. Since no one listened, the angry prisoners suddenly decided to call attention to their grievances by staging a work and hunger strike.

The strike embarrassed and infuriated the Warden. The guards and civilian staff were extremely alarmed by the strike, fearing that the protest might escalate to the point of violence. The guards and civilian staff, even before the strike, have been aware that their means of protection from the prisoners—as well as their equipment and supplies in general—were inadequate.

At first, the Warden had hoped that the strike would fall apart from lack of organization. Soon, however, he found that the inmates were united and would end the strike, temporarily, only if he agreed to call in governor-appointed mediators to investigate the situation at the prison.

In preparation for the mediators' visit, the Warden has prepared a background statement on Medford Correctional Facility. Also, the prisoners have asked that the mediators receive a copy of the "Medford Correctional Facility Prisoner Orientation." (Both items are given on the following pages.) Before deciding what to recommend to settle the dispute, the mediators have called an open meeting so that they can hear from the prisoners, representatives of the Warden's office, the guards, and the civilian staff. One thing is certain—the conclusions reached at the open meeting will be important, for all parties know that if the dispute is not settled quickly, the inmates will resume their disruptive, dangerous strike.

A BACKGROUND STATEMENT: MEDFORD CORRECTIONAL FACILITY

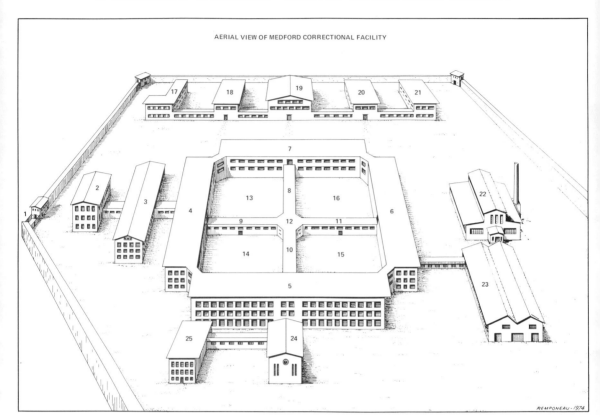

AERIAL VIEW OF MEDFORD CORRECTIONAL FACILITY

REMPONEAU - 1974

1 Front Gate	10 B Catwalk and Tunnel	18 Hospital
2 Administration Bldg.	11 C Catwalk and Tunnel	19 Mess/Kitchen/Bake Shop
3 Commissary/Garage	12 Grand Central Station	20 Laundry
4 A Block	13 D Yard	21 State Shop
5 B Block	14 A Yard	22 Powerhouse
6 C Block	15 B Yard	23 Metal Shops
7 D Block	16 C Yard	24 Auditorium/Chapel
8 D Catwalk and Tunnel	17 Reception Center and	25 School
9 A Catwalk and Tunnel	Segregation Cells	

Opened in 1935, Medford Correctional Facility is one
of fifteen such facilities in the state. Medford,
which houses 2,000 inmates, operates at a cost of
over $8,000,000 a year. Its correctional staff of
345 includes the Warden, his deputies, 5 lieutenants,
7 sergeants, and 360 regular guards. The 135 civilian
workers provide the facility with services in such
areas as: industry, education, religion, health, coun-
seling, parole, and plant operation.

YEARLY EXPENDITURES

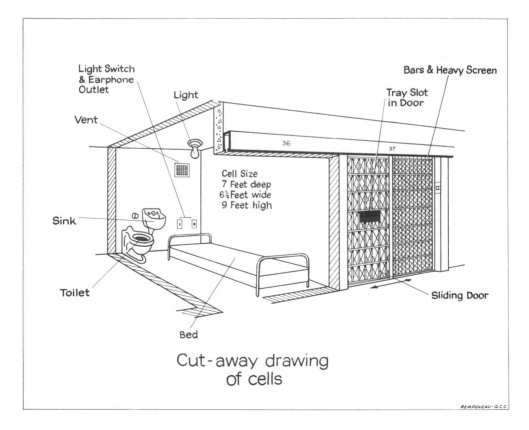

62%
Correction
officers' salaries

7%
Food

5% Inmates' wages

3%

3% Medical care

2% Clothing

Education
and guidance

18%
Facility
maintenance

100% = $8,000,000.

Light Switch
& Earphone
Outlet

Light

Vent

Bars & Heavy Screen

Tray Slot
in Door

Cell Size
7 Feet deep
6½ Feet wide
9 Feet high

36

37

Sink

Toilet

Bed

Sliding Door

Cut-away drawing
of cells

REMPONEAU-Q.C.C.

9

MEDFORD CORRECTIONAL FACILITY PRISONER ORIENTATION

DAILY SCHEDULE

6:30 A.M. -- Breakfast (juice, cereal, bread, coffee)

7:00 A.M. -- Return to cell

11:00 A.M. -- Recreation in yard

12 noon -- Lunch, (meat, potato or rice, vegetable, bread, coffee)

12:30 P.M. -- Report to work or to school

5:30 P.M. -- Supper (soup, bread, milk or coffee)

5:50 P.M. -- Return to cell

8:00 P.M. -- No talking allowed in cells after this hour

11:00 P.M. -- Lights out

Clothes: All provided by the state. Shirts and sweaters must be tucked in; shirts must be fully buttoned except for top button.

Health: State provides per inmate 1 comb, 1 towel, and each month 1 bar of soap.

Shower: 1 per week

Wash up: 2 qts. hot water to cell each afternoon

Hair: No moustaches; sideburns no longer than 1-1/2"

Doctor: 2 available Monday through Friday, 8 to 11 A.M.

Dentist: 2 available Monday through Friday, 9 A.M. to 3 P.M.

(Note: Be prepared to speak with medical personnel through a wire screen; physical examinations available only when doctor or dentist deems it necessary.)

Prison Store: 1 visit per inmate every two weeks; prices as at outside stores. Available: candy, cigarettes, instant coffee and soup, toiletries, writing materials, etc.

Education: 5 teachers available; inmates are paid 25¢ a day to attend classes. Courses: basic reading and math up to high school equivalency; vocational training in auto mechanics, barbering, carpentry, drafting, printing, and typing; 14-week Dale Carnegie Institute course in public speaking and self-confidence.

Work: Inmates placed in jobs, unless they attend school; pay is 25¢ to $1.00 a day, depending on experience.
Jobs include: carpenter, clerk, farm worker, janitor, kitchen helper, laundry worker, messenger, metal shop worker, painter, plumber.

*uprising
behind
bars*

Mail:

Only from, and to, approved list of relatives; all mail censored. Packages: limit of 15 lb.; cannot contain glass jars, cans over 2 lb. or pressurized, combs over 6" long.

Recreation:

TV: 1 set in yard.
Radio: on earphones; 3 stations in each cell.

Visits:

All visits held in rooms with visitation screens; physical contact between inmate and visitor forbidden. Permitted visitors: immediate family, clergymen, lawyers (all others must apply 10 days in advance).

Religion:

Chapel services provided for: Catholics, Christian Scientists, Jehovah's Witnesses, Jews, and a few Protestant sects.

WARNING:

VIOLATION OF PRISON RULES WILL LEAD TO KEEPLOCK (NOT ALLOWED OUT OF CELL) OR TO SPECIAL SEGREGATION CELLS (CONTACT WITH OTHER PRISONERS FORBIDDEN)

In all cases, a guard's decision is final; guard decides if a prison rule, written here or otherwise in practice, has been broken.

the roles

PRISONER

As an inmate at Medford Correctional Facility, you and your fellow inmates have been complaining for quite a while about living conditions and rules at the prison. Recently, also, escalating tensions between guards and prisoners have made you fear for your own safety. In addition, although you realize that the teachers and job supervisors are doing the best they can with their limited supplies and materials, you feel that neither the education available nor the jobs assigned in prison are preparing you for your eventual return to society. Because no one has listened to your complaints, you and the other inmates went on a work and hunger strike. You agreed to end the strike temporarily only when the Warden consented to call in outside mediators appointed by the governor. Now the mediators have called an open meeting for the airing of all complaints, and you must be ready to present your views, backed up by references to specific aspects of the prison situation. (If there is more than one person in your role-group, select a leader.)

PRISON GUARD

As a Guard at Medford Correctional Facility, you were greatly angered and frightened by the recent inmate strike. You feel that prisoners should not have a say in how they are treated, for most of the inmates are beyond rehabilitation—after all, more than 70 percent of the prisoners were incarcerated at least once before in their lives. Your key concern is that the number of prisoners has sharply increased in the last few years, but the number of guards has remained the same. This, combined with the problem of very old-fashioned security equipment, makes you uneasy about your safety. You are not convinced that the Warden is doing all that he can, and you and your fellow guards have recently threatened a job action unless you are given more adequate protection from the inmates. At the open meeting, you want to present your views about the situation at Medford. (If there is more than one person in your role-group, select a leader.)

WARDEN AND DEPUTY

As the Warden or his Deputy, you are extremely irritated that there has been a strike and that you have had to call in outside mediators to work things out. You are also aware that the guards and civilian staff have threatened a job action unless their safety from harm by the inmates is protected by more up-to-date surveillance and alarm systems. At the open meeting, you hope to be able to convince the mediators that it is not the purpose of a prison to coddle lawbreakers. Also, you will try to show the mediators that given the limited budget and space available for the prison, the Warden's office is doing the best possible job. (If there is more than one person in your role-group, select a leader.)

CIVILIAN STAFF MEMBER

You are a Civilian Staff Member, one of a large group that includes teachers, medical personnel, prison job supervisors, correction counselors, parole officers, and clergymen. You sympathize with many of the prisoners' complaints, but the recent strike has led you to worry about your personal safety. During normal times, you have always thought of yourself as willing to help inmates with their problems, and you are keenly aware that you have been hindered by inadequate facilities—classroom materials are old, work equipment is obsolete, even medical and secretarial supplies are limited. Nevertheless, you feel that without better protection from danger, you and your fellow civilian staff members will have to stage a job action. At the open meeting, you want to argue for better conditions for the prisoners so that the threat of violence will be reduced. (If there is more than one person in your role-group, select a leader.)

MEDIATOR

You are a Mediator appointed by the governor to investigate conditions at Medford Correctional Facility and to make recommendations for settling the dispute now going on. At the open meeting you have called, you want to give all sides a chance to air their views. (If there is more than one person in your role-group, select a leader.) After someone has spoken from each group, you can allow, and also freely participate in, a general discussion of the situation. Try to get the entire group to work out a possible solution. When you make your final recommendations to the governor, you have to keep one important point in mind—the governor is eager to keep state spending down and he is likely to be against proposing legislation that will increase the state budget for prisons.

communication actions

running a simulation-game

In "Uprising Behind Bars" each role is taken by, or given to, a different person—or, if possible, group of persons. The idea is to involve as many people as possible. For ease of identification, each person writes his or her role-title on a name tag (blanks available p. 143) and pins it on. Next, the Situation Statement is read aloud by the teacher or a student, and the action is started by all members of each separate role-group getting together to read the rest of the "Uprising Behind Bars" materials and to plan what they will say at the open meeting called by the Mediator(s). To help communication during the simulation-game, each person can use a Simulation-Game Work Sheet at the back of the book. Next, everyone is called together by the Mediator(s) for the open meeting where the participants informally act out what they think would go on at such a meeting. Finally, the role-group responsible for making a decision confers and announces its ruling.

sharpening skills

In addition to running a simulation-game by informally acting out "Uprising Behind Bars," you can use the materials in the simulation-game as a basis for sharpening your skills in the four areas related to effective communication in English: speaking, listening, reading, and writing.

SPEAKING ACTIONS

1. Take the role of any of the people in "Uprising Behind Bars." Assume that you have been given a chance to air your views on a local television community-affairs program. Develop the speech you would give. As you do so, remember that the television viewers do not know anything about what has been going on at Medford Correctional Facility. Therefore, be sure to include specific supporting arguments to whatever is your point of view.

2. Suppose that you are one of the governor-appointed mediators. Assume that you have just come from an open meeting at Medford Correctional Facility where you have learned about the many problems that exist there. Now you find that you must go before a state legislature budget committee to plea for more funds for the prison. Develop the speech you would give. As you do so, remember that the members of the state legislature do not know

specifics of Medford Correctional Facility. You should also keep in mind that state moneys are usually scarce, especially for unpopular causes, and in most states prisoners do not have the vote.

3. Suppose that you are an expert on various types of state correctional facilities. Assume that you have been invited to give a speech to a meeting of state wardens and their representatives. You have been asked to speak about what you consider to be the ideal conditions for a prison. Develop the speech you would give. As you do so, remember that you can make up whatever setup you think would be best for the proper treatment and "correction" of prisoners.

4. Suppose that you are the prisoner in the last photograph shown in "Uprising Behind Bars." Prepare a three- to five-minute monologue of what you might be saying to yourself as you are standing there.

5. Be prepared to defend or oppose any of the following debate topics:
   (a) Prisoners should be punished, not rehabilitated.
   (b) Crime is the fault of the society, not the individual.
   (c) Never hire an ex-convict.
   (d) Crime does not pay.

LISTENING ACTIONS

1. Ask someone who has been in prison about the conditions there. (If you do not know anyone who has been in prison, ask people you know to assume that they were once prison inmates.) Compare what you hear with what you have read in "Uprising Behind Bars." Listen to the responses you get not only for factual content but also for underlying attitudes, especially as expressed by "loaded language."

2. Ask a prison guard his or her opinion of prisons and or prisoners in general. (If you do not know a prison guard, ask people you know to assume that they are prison guards.) Compare what you hear with the opinions and attitudes of the guards in "Uprising Behind Bars." Listen to the responses you get not only for factual content but also for underlying attitudes, especially as expressed by "loaded language."

3. Take a poll among 15–20 people by asking them if they would be willing to pay higher state taxes in order to provide better conditions for prisoners. As you listen to the answers, try to hear not only the specific answer but also general underlying attitudes about prisoners and prisons. As you take your poll, take brief notes and then see if you can discern patterns in the answers.

4. Be on the alert for special television programs about prison conditions, prisoners, prison reform ideas, and so forth. As you hear the statements of various people, try to become aware of underlying attitudes as well as specific content.

communication actions

Reread "Uprising Behind Bars," following the SQ3R (Survey, Question, Read, Review, Recite) approach discussed in the Reading section in the chapter on communication skills at the back of this book. The SQ3R approach will make it much easier for you to become familiar with all the material in "Uprising Behind Bars."

Detailed Reading and Reacting

Here are questions that call upon your ability to read for main idea, major details, inferences (getting at underlying attitudes), and then to form your own opinions. Sharp skills in these four reading areas will help you to be an expert reader.

I. *Main Idea*
    A. What has caused the serious crisis to develop at Medford Correctional Facility?
    B. What is your general idea of a prison as it is described in the Background Statement on Medford Correctional Facility?
    C. What is your general idea of the life of a prisoner as it is described in the Prisoner Orientation?
    D. What is the point of view of each of the separate roles?

II. *Major Details*
    A. The Situation Statement
        1. Why were the guards and civilian staff alarmed by the strike?
        2. Why was an open meeting called?
    B. The Background Statement: Medford Correctional Facility
        1. How many inmates and how many non-inmates are there in the prison?
        2. Read the pie graph. What is the overall cost of running the prison, and how much money is allotted to which separate expense areas?
        3. What are the major types of buildings at Medford Correctional Facility?
    C. The Medford Correctional Facility Prisoner Orientation
        1. How many hours do the prisoners remain in their cells?
        2. What courses are offered at the prison, and how many teachers are there?
        3. How much pay are the prisoners given?
        4. For what religions are prayer services offered?

III. *Inference*
    A. The Situation Statement
        Why did the strike embarrass the Warden?
    B. The Background Statement: Medford Correctional Facility
        What is the implied attitude toward prisoners shown by the cell?

C. The Medford Correctional Facility Prisoner Orientation
   1. What is the implied attitude toward prisoners shown by the schedule and the rules and regulations?
   2. What is the effect of the "warning" given?
D. The Photographs
   What feeling about prison life is each photograph meant to give?
E. The Roles
   1. What is the Warden's implied attitude in his use of the phrase "not to coddle lawbreakers"?
   2. What is the guards' implied attitude toward prisoners when they say "prisoners should not have a say in how they are treated"?
   3. Why does the Mediator want the *entire group* to try to work out a possible solution?

IV. *Opinion*
   A. What do you think about conditions at Medford Correctional Facility?
   B. In general, do you think that protest strikes are helpful (a) to call immediate attention to a situation; (b) to change things in the long run? Why or why not?

Vocabulary Study   Here are some words you have read in "Uprising Behind Bars." (They are listed in the order in which they appeared.) Do you know the meaning of each? For a discussion of how to study vocabulary, look at the Reading section of the chapter on communication skills at the back of this book.

crisis
grievances
infuriate
escalate . . . escalating
mediators
orientation
dispute
disruptive
facility
expenditures
surveillance
coddle
rehabilitation
incarcerated
obsolete
legislation

Additional Reading 1. Look under "prison" in the card catalog of your college or public library. Take out some books written by prisoners and some written by wardens. Compare their points of view.

2. Be on the alert for newspaper and magazine articles and editorials about prisons, prison conditions, prison reform, prisoners, etc. Compare and contrast the details given to those you read about in "Uprising Behind Bars."

WRITING ACTIONS

As a result of taking part in the simulation-game "Uprising Behind Bars" (or just reading it), you can probably think of many ideas to write about. Below are some suggestions for both paragraph and essay topics. The topics range from those directly related to "Uprising Behind Bars" to those on the general subject of prisons and crime. For your convenience, any topic that fits into one or more of the rhetorical forms mentioned in the Writing section of the chapter on communication skills at the back of this book is followed by one or more of these symbols in parentheses: D for description; N for narration; Def. for definition; P for process; R for report; and A&P for argument and persuasion.

Paragraph Writing 1. Do you agree with the prisoners who are complaining? Write a paragraph in which you express and support your point of view. (A&P)

2. How would you solve the problems at Medford Correctional Facility? Write a paragraph in which you present your solution. (P)

3. Many authorities say that the family of a prisoner is very important in a prisoner's rehabilitation. Write a paragraph in which you consider the reasons behind this point of view. (A&P, P)

4. Should the guards in a prison be of the same ethnic and racial background as the prisoners? Write a paragraph in which you state and support your opinion. (A&P)

5. Write a paragraph in which you comment on this quote: "Purposelessness is the fruitful mother of crime." (Charles Parkhurst) (D, A&P)

Essay Writing 1. Write a position paper in which you express your opinion about the situation at Medford Correctional Facility. Follow the position paper pattern given in the Writing section of the chapter on communication skills at the back of this book. Assume that your paper will be read by the governor who wants to work out a solution. (R, A&P)

2. What is your idea of a prison? Write an essay in which you define your point of view. Some of the ideas you might want to consider are: What is the purpose of a prison? What should life be like for prisoners? What should the released prisoner be like? (Def.)

3. How do you feel when you look closely at the third photograph in "Uprising Behind Bars"? Study it carefully and then write an essay in which you describe the scene. As you do so, remember to try to give the reader the mood and feeling as well as the specific contents of the scene. To make your description as effective as possible, be sure to refer to the five senses (sight, hearing, touch, taste, and smell) as you write. (D)

4. Do you think that prisoners should have civil rights like those of all other citizens? Write an essay in which you discuss your point of view. Some of the ideas you might want to consider are: mail censorship, minimum wages, religious freedom, guards' decisions not subject to review, chances for education, control over visitations. (A&P)

5. How do you think the rehabilitation of prisoners is best done? Write an essay in which you discuss your ideas on this subject. As you do so, you might want to keep in mind that almost all prisoners are eventually returned to society—and that from 70 percent to 80 percent soon commit other crimes and go back to prison. You might also want to consider the new "prison furlough" system that allows nonviolent criminals to spend various periods of time in the outside world so that they can work, or go to school, or spend time with their families. (P)

6. Do you ever wonder what has led someone to become a criminal? Is he or she basically bad, or have events caused the problem? Was the particular crime planned or did it happen almost by accident? Write a narrative essay in which you make up the story of someone's life and show how it led to prison. (N)

7. Do you think female prisoners should be treated in the same manner in which male prisoners are? Write an essay in which you present your point of view. Some of the questions you might want to consider are: Should female prisoners be treated more gently than male prisoners? Should female prisoners be allowed to have brightly decorated cells or dormitories when male prisoners cannot? If a female prisoner has a baby after she arrives in prison, should she be forced to give up the baby for adoption or should she be allowed to keep it in prison? (A&P)

8. Do you think that capital punishment is a deterrent to crime? Write an essay in which you discuss your opinion. You might want to give a brief history of the use of capital punishment so that your opinion is grounded in experience. You might also want to discuss which crimes, if any, you think should be considered capital punishment offenses. (A&P, D)

9. Read through the speaking, listening, and opinion reading questions given for "Uprising Behind Bars." Write an essay on any one of the topics that interests you.

10. Here are some statements about prisons, crime, and so forth. Select one statement that interests you and develop an essay around it: (A&P, Def., P)
    (a) A prison is a wall built around problems.
    (b) "The prison system is the only business which can succeed by its own failures: It needs men returning to the fold so that it can perpetuate itself." (Herman Badillo)
    (c) "All crime is a disease and should be treated as such." (Mahatma Gandhi)
    (d) Society prepares the crime; the criminal commits it.

taxis
for sale

a simulation-game for English about buying the ideal taxicab

the roles

(5 to 35)

TAXICAB "B" SALESPERSON

TAXICAB "C" SALESPERSON

TAXICAB "P" SALESPERSON

MID-CITY TAXICAB EXECUTIVE

TAXICAB DRIVER

the situation

The Mid-City Taxicab Company wants to buy a fleet of seventy-five taxis to replace cars that are getting old. Because a large investment of money is involved, the Mid-City Taxicab Company wants to make sure that it is getting the best product for its money.

The fleet-sales department of each of three taxicab manufacturers is eager to sell its taxi to the Mid-City Taxicab Company. Each of the three taxicab manufacturers, known as "B," "C," and "P," has prepared a sales brochure that presents the key facts and advantages of its product. (A copy of each sales brochure is given on the following pages.) By comparing his or her product to the others available, each Taxicab Salesperson hopes to promote the sale and thereby earn a 2 percent commission and further job security. The salespeople know that in making a selection, the Executives of the Mid-City Taxicab Company will consider many factors: economy of operation, dependability, and attractiveness to customers and drivers.

Satisfying drivers has become an important consideration in taxicab purchases, for with the increase in crimes against taxicab drivers and the long hours necessary on the job, all taxicab fleet owners are having trouble finding good drivers. Men and women who are willing to drive taxis have become more demanding, not only in their concern for safety but also in their concern for driver comfort and a minimum of car breakdowns.

In order to learn more about the three taxicabs available, the Executives of the Mid-City Taxicab Company have called a meeting so that the salespeople from each manufacturer can be heard and so that the representatives of the drivers can react to each product. The final purchase decisions of the Mid-City Taxicab Company will be crucial for company income and driver satisfaction for the next few years.

TAXICAB "B"

WITH THE SLEEK, MODERN STYLING AND COMFORT
THAT ATTRACT CUSTOMERS!

- **Power Steering**
- **Power front disc brakes**
- **Turbo Hydra-matic Transmission**
- **350 cubic-inch V8 engine**
- **Seats four comfortably**
- **Thirty-nine inches of backseat legroom**
- **Thirty-eight inches of backseat headroom**
- **Interior trimmed in cloth/vinyl**
- **Large rear trunk for luggage**
- **121½-inch wheelbase**
- **Bumper system that retracts on minor impact and hydraulically cushions the shock**
- **Energy-absorbing steering column**
- **Windshield glass so strong that in tests it was undamaged by a one-ounce steel ball hitting the windshield at 50 miles an hour**
- **Steel side-guard door beams**

- **Heavy-duty full foam seats**
- **Power ventilation system with three-speed blower**
- **Durable shock absorbers for consistent ride control**
- **Just $4000 per car**
- **A variety of optional features at extra cost:**
   - **Air conditioning**
   - **Tinted glass**
   - **Partition to separate driver from passenger**
   - **Front and rear bumper guards**
   - **Power door-lock system**
   - **Comfortilt steering wheel**
   - **Rear window defogger**
   - **Steel-belted radial ply white stripe tires**
   - **Power windows**

TAXICAB "C"

SINCE 1922, THE TAXI WITH PROVEN DEPENDABILITY!

- Power Steering
- Power front disc brakes
- Dual range automatic transmission
- 250 cubic-inch six-cylinder engine
- Seats six with optional rear auxiliary seats in position
- Forty-eight inches of backseat legroom
- Thirty-five inches of backseat headroom
- Roomy trunk for increased luggage space
- Impact-absorbing steering column
- Meets current emission control requirements
- 120-inch wheelbase
- Entire cab lined with steel
- Interchangeable front and rear bumpers for easy repairs

- Higher, wider door openings for easier entry and exit
- Energy-absorbing bumpers
- Safety plate glass in all windows
- Heavy-duty shock absorbers
- Just $4300 per car
- A variety of optional features at extra cost:
    - Air conditioning
    - Rear auxiliary seats
    - Rear window defogger
    - Life-Guard partition to enclose driver's compartment
    - Tinted glass
    - V-8 engine
    - Power rear door locks

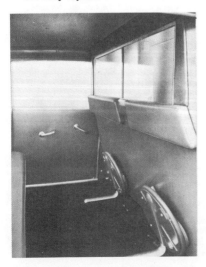

TAXICAB "P"

THE TAXI OF THE FUTURE IS HERE TODAY!

- Seats four comfortably

- Five-foot-high doors for easy entry

- Sixty-four inches of backseat legroom

- Forty-five inches of backseat headroom

- Ramp for passengers in wheelchairs

- Luggage in full view on special platform next to driver

- Flat floor

- Only two inches longer than a Volkswagen but with more headroom and legroom than a Cadillac limousine

- Low pollution engine (rear mounted)

- Removable engine and drive-train system for quick and easy maintenance

- One hundred-eight-inch wheelbase for easy maneuverability

- Fully enclosed driver's compartment

- Posture-form adjustable seat for driver

- Air conditioning and ventilation system under driver's control

- Separate air conditioning controls for passengers

- Safety padded passenger compartment

- Easy to park

- Long anticipated life

- Lower operating cost

- Less room on streets

- Quicker movement in traffic

- Easy cornering

- Just $4100 per car

the roles

**TAXICAB "B"
SALESPERSON**

Taxicab "B" is a car familiar to everyone because it is a regular automobile with slight additions and changes to make it a taxicab. It is the most commonly used taxicab on the streets. You hope to be able to persuade the Mid-City Taxicab Company to select taxicab "B" for its fleet purchase of seventy-five taxis. In preparing your case for presentation at the coming open meeting, you will want to refer to the three sales brochures given so that by comparing taxicab "B" to the other taxis available, you can praise your product and put the other two in a lesser light. (If there is more than one person in your role-group, select a leader.)

**TAXICAB "C"
SALESPERSON**

Taxicab "C" is a car designed especially to be a taxi; it is not a regular automobile slightly changed for taxicab purposes. It has been available for many years and it has proven itself well-suited to its job. You hope to be able to persuade the Mid-City Taxicab Company to select taxicab "C" for its fleet purchase of seventy-five taxis. In preparing your case for presentation at the coming open sales meeting, you will want to refer to the three sales brochures given so that by comparing taxicab "C" to the other taxis available, you can praise your product and put the other two in a lesser light. (If there is more than one person in your role-group, select a leader.)

**TAXICAB "P"
SALESPERSON**

Taxicab "P" is a revolutionary new taxi designed with special safety and environmental features. Called the "people taxi" by its inventors, the "P" taxi is designed especially for city use. You hope to be able to persuade the Mid-City Taxicab Company to select taxicab "P" for its fleet purchase of seventy-five taxis. In preparing your case for the coming open sales meeting, you will want to refer to the three sales brochures given so that by comparing taxicab "P" to the other taxis available, you can praise your product and put the other two in a lesser light. (If there is more than one person in your role-group, select a leader.)

**MID-CITY
TAXICAB
EXECUTIVE**

You have an important decision to make. You must decide which of three taxicabs your company should select for its fleet purchase of seventy-five taxis. You want to make a sensible, economical selection that you think will appeal to drivers and to customers. You have to evaluate each of the three cars by reading the sales brochures, listening to the salesperson from each manufacturer, and by asking the opinion of the drivers' representatives.

It is up to you to conduct an open sales meeting so that you can hear from all manufacturers and the drivers. (If there is more than one person in your role-group, select a leader.) After a salesperson from each manufacturer and the drivers have presented their views, you can ask questions and allow a general discussion. Then you must make your final decision.

**TAXICAB
DRIVER**

You have been driving taxicabs in the city for many years. No matter which taxicab fleet company you work for, your salary is determined by union rules, not by the individual company. Your concern, therefore, is to work for a taxicab fleet company that has safe, dependable taxis that will attract customers. One of your key concerns is your safety from robbery and other crimes that often occur in urban taxicabs. In preparing to attend the open sales meeting called by the Executives of the Mid-City Taxicab Company, you will want to refer to the sales brochures given and to prepare a list of features you think important in taxicabs. Then, after you have heard the sales presentation of each of the three taxicab manufacturers, you will want to make your recommendations for fleet purchase. (If there is more than one person in your role-group, select a leader.)

communication actions

running a simulation-game

In "Taxis For Sale" each role is taken by, or given to, a different person —or, if possible, group of persons. The idea is to try to involve as many people as possible. For ease of identification, each person writes his or her role-title on a name tag (blanks available p. 143) and pins it on. Next, the Situation Statement is read aloud by the teacher or a student, and the action is started by all members of each separate role-group getting together to read the rest of the "Taxis For Sale" materials and to plan what they will say at the sales meeting called by the Mid-City Taxicab Company Executive(s). To help communication during the simulation-game, each person can use a Simulation-Game Work Sheet at the back of the book. Next, everyone is called together by the Mid-City Taxicab Executive(s) for the sales meeting where the participants informally act out what they think would go on at such a meeting. Finally, the role-group responsible for making a decision confers and announces its ruling.

sharpening skills

In addition to running a simulation-game by informally acting out "Taxis For Sale," you can use the materials in the simulation-game as a basis for sharpening your skills in the four areas related to effective communication in English: speaking, listening, reading, and writing.

SPEAKING ACTIONS

1. Take the role of the salesperson of any of the three taxis in "Taxis For Sale." Assume that you have to sell the taxi not for fleet purchase but to an individual owner. Develop the sales speech you would give. As you do so, remember that the individual owner is investing his or her own money, not that of a large company, and is planning to drive the taxi himself or herself.

2. Suppose that you are the mayor of a large city and you must announce to the public that private automobile traffic and much commercial traffic will be banned from the center of the city. Assume that you have to make this announcement in the form of a speech given on television. Develop the speech you would give. As you do so, remember not only to state the new regulations but also to explain the reasons behind them.

3. Be prepared to defend or oppose any one of the following debate topics:
   (a) The automobile enhances life.
   (b) "For over half a century the automobile has brought death, injury, and the most inestimable sorrow and deprivation to millions of people." (Ralph Nader)
   (c) "Men have become tools of their tools." (Henry Thoreau)

LISTENING ACTIONS

1. Ask someone who drives a taxicab what features he or she thinks would constitute the ideal taxicab. (If you cannot arrange to speak to someone who drives a taxicab, ask people you know to assume that they drive a taxicab.) Compare what you hear with the features of the three taxicabs in "Taxis For Sale." Which of the three would you try to sell the driver you spoke with?

2. Ask someone who does a great deal of driving in a large city what problems are caused by traffic congestion. (If you do not know someone who does this sort of driving, ask people you know to assume they do.) Listen to the responses you get not only for factual content but also for underlying awareness of the difficulties involved in trying to solve the increasing problem of crowded highways and city streets.

3. Take a poll among 15–20 car owners by asking them what improvements, if any, in mass transportation would make them willing to leave their cars at home. As you listen to the answers you get, try to hear not only the factual content but also the underlying attitudes toward car ownership and public willingness to sacrifice convenience for the good of the community. As you take your poll, take brief notes and then see if you can discern patterns in the answers.

READING ACTIONS

SQ3R

Reread "Taxis For Sale," following the SQ3R (Survey, Question, Read, Review, Recite) approach discussed in the Reading section in the chapter on communication skills at the back of this book. The SQ3R approach will make it easier for you to become familiar with all the material in "Taxis For Sale."

Detailed Reading and Reacting

Here are questions that call upon your ability to read for main idea, major details, inferences (getting at underlying attitudes), and then to form your own opinions. Sharp skills in these four reading areas will help you to be an expert reader.

I. **Main Idea**
   A. What is the purpose of the sales meeting?
   B. What do the sales brochures show?
   C. What does the photograph at the beginning of the simulation-game show?

II. **Major Details**
   A. The Situation Statement
      1. Why does the Mid-City Taxicab Company have to purchase seventy-five taxis?
      2. What does the company look for in a taxi?
      3. Why are the drivers' opinions about the taxicab selection important?
   B. The Sales Brochures
      Compare the three available taxicabs. What are the differences in their motor sizes, standard features, and costs?

III. **Inference**
   The Roles
      1. What is implied about a taxi that is "slightly changed" from a regular automobile to be a taxi?
      2. Why is the "P" taxicab called the "people taxi"?

IV. **Opinion**
   A. Which taxicab would you select for the Mid-City Taxicab Company fleet purchase?
   B. What features are most important to you in a car?

Vocabulary Study

Here are some words you have read in "Taxis For Sale." (They are listed in the order in which they appeared.) Do you know the meaning of each? For a discussion of how to study vocabulary, look at the Reading section of the chapter on communication skills at the back of this book.

fleet	absorbers	safety plate
brochure	optional	tinted
dependability	partition	limousine
disc	defogger	maintenance
transmission	radial	maneuverability
wheelbase	cylinder	anticipated
hydraulically	auxiliary	environmental
ventilation	emission	urban
durable	interchangeable	

Additional Reading

1. Look under "automobile" in the card catalog of your college or public library. See if there are any books about taxicabs or about automobiles of the future. Compare what you read with the information in "Taxis For Sale."

2. Be on the alert for newspaper and magazine articles and editorials about taxicab drivers, urban traffic problems and the like. Begin to formulate your ideas about the issues raised.

WRITING ACTIONS

As a result of taking part in the simulation-game "Taxis For Sale" (or just reading it), you can probably think of many ideas to write about. Below are some suggestions for both paragraph and essay topics. The topics range from those directly related to "Taxis For Sale" to those on the general topic of pollution, conservation, and ecology. For your convenience, any topic that fits into one or more of the rhetorical forms mentioned in the Writing section of the chapter on communication skills at the back of this book is followed by one or more of these symbols in parentheses: D for description; N for narration; Def. for definition; P for process; R for report; and A&P for argument and persuasion.

Paragraph Writing

1. Which taxicab do you think is best suited to be a taxicab? Write a paragraph in which you present and support your opinion. (A&P, D)

2. Taxicab drivers have become an easy target for crimes such as robbery and murder. What might the taxicab manufacturers include in the taxicabs to insure the safety of the drivers? Write a paragraph in which you present and explain your suggestions. (A&P, D)

3. Bus transportation is an important part of urban as well as rural transportation. One type of bus is the school bus, used to transport millions of schoolchildren each day. Do you think automobile safety requirements such as seat belts and cushioned interiors should be required in buses? Write a paragraph in which you present and support your opinion. (A&P)

4. Should car pools be required by law in crowded cities or should automobiles with only one occupant be allowed without restriction? Write a paragraph in which you present and support your opinion. (A&P)

Essay Writing

1. Assume that as chief of purchasing it is your responsibility to recommend to the president of Mid-City Taxicab Company which taxicab to buy. Write an essay as a memo of recommendation that analyzes the company's needs, the available taxicabs, and the best choice for the company. (A&P)

2. What types of public transportation are available in your community? Can you think of how you would like to see the mass transportation system improved? Write an essay in which you describe the ideal mass transportation system for your community. As you do so, you might want to include not only improvement of existing facilities but also introduction of new types of mass transportation such as, if appropriate, the monorail and the hydrofoil. (D, A&P, P)

3. If you could buy a new car right now, which of all the cars in the world would you select? Write an essay in which you describe your favorite car. As you do so, remember not only to list its features but also to tell why you think the features are important. (D)

4. What makes certain people pick certain kinds of cars? Some observers say that one look at the make, model, year, and color of a car and its owner is completely revealed. Do you agree? Write an essay in which you make observations about people's selections for cars. As you do so, try to include not only descriptions of cars and their owners but also your ideas about the possible reasons people make the choices they do. (D, R, and A&P)

5. Read through the speaking, listening, and reading opinion questions given for "Taxis For Sale." Write an essay on any one of the topics that interests you.

6. Is a car a luxury or a necessity in today's world? Could we get along without cars? If not, what can be done about the growing congestion on the highways? Write an essay in which you discuss your opinion about the needs for cars. As you do so, remember not only to think about your own feelings but also about the impact of the automobile on the world at large. (A&P)

7. Here are some statements about automobiles and about machines in general. Select one statement that interests you and develop an essay around it. (A&P)

   (a) "The automobile has not merely taken over the street, it has dissolved the living tissue of the city. . . . Gas filled, noisy and hazardous, our streets have become the most inhuman landscape in the world." (James Fitch)

   (b) "As machines get to be more and more like men, men will come to be more like machines." (Joseph Wood Krutch)

   (c) "A tool is but the extension of a man's hand, and a machine is but a complex tool. He that invents a machine augments the power of man and the well-being of mankind." (Henry Ward Beecher)

conservation crisis

a simulation-game for English
about the impact of pollution on a small town

the roles
(6 to 36)

CONSERVATIONIST

MEMBER OF THE
DEPARTMENT
OF ENVIRONMENTAL
CONSERVATION

TOWN RESIDENT—
FACTORY WORKER

TOWN RESIDENT—
UNEMPLOYED MALE

TOWN RESIDENT—
RESTAURANT OWNER

PARSONS CHEMICAL
COMPANY EXECUTIVE

the
situation

Destruction of ecological balances has escalated dangerously in
Surfside, an American town located on the shores of a saltwater inlet
called Great Bay. Surfside has long been known for its beautiful
beaches, excellent fishing, and natural bird sanctuary, all of which
once attracted tourists from hundreds of miles away. These tourists
brought business to the community, benefiting the shops and restaurants as well as the local marina and boat stations. All of this has been
spoiled by the enormous amount of liquid pollutants that Parsons
Chemical Company empties daily into Great Bay. Parsons Chemical
possesses a Discharge Permit, issued by the state's Department of
Environmental Conservation, that allows the factory to dump its
wastes into the water. But as a result of the heavy pollution, few
fish remain in the water, few birds take sanctuary in the now greatly
defoliated marshland, and few people dare swim from the beaches.
However, Parsons Chemical Company is Surfside's largest industry.
It employs a substantial part of the town's population and it pays a
good proportion of the local real estate taxes that support the munici-
pal government and its services.

In an effort to save their environment, a group of conservationists and
other town residents have petitioned the state Department of Environmental Conservation to modify Parsons' Discharge Permit. The citizens want the Discharge Permit to be rewritten to allow only the
barest minimum of pollutant output necessary after automated waste
disposal. The Department of Environmental Conservation has
responded to the citizens' request by calling a public hearing in Surfside to give all the people involved an opportunity to present their
complaints and recommendations. In preparation for this hearing,
Surfside's Chamber of Commerce has compiled a fact sheet to aid
everyone's understanding of the scope of the town's problem. (A copy
of the fact sheet is given on the next page.) Without a doubt, the
public hearing about to be held will have a significant impact on the
future of Surfside.

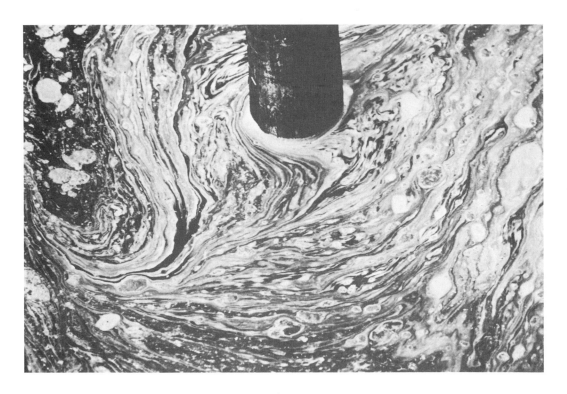

FACT SHEET ABOUT SURFSIDE

Prepared by the Chamber of Commerce of Surfside

Location: A choice spot on Great Bay which is a saltwater inlet known for its excellent fishing, beautiful beaches, and fine bird sanctuary in its marshland.

The Working Population:

Store and small business operators. 100

Office and store employees (white collar) . . .150

Parsons Chemical executives (white collar). . . 10

Parsons Chemical factory workers (blue collar) 300

Doctors, lawyers, dentists. 50

Marina and boat station employees 15

Civil servants and politicians. 50

Unemployed. 50

Note: Among this group are fifty conservationists who are deeply worried about the pollution problem

Business Information:

*Parsons Chemical Company, which has its factory on
the shore of Great Bay, dumps all of its chemical
wastes into the bay. The company employs more than
any other business in town. Also, Parsons Chemical
pays a large share of the local real estate taxes
and gives generously to the town's library, hospital,
and three major religious groups.

*Some of the town's smaller businesses are a branch
bank, a marina, two small boat stations, two large
supermarkets, ten restaurants and bars, and twenty
small shops. The lack of tourists recently has made
business fall by 40 percent this year. In general, the number of tourists is 75 percent smaller
than last year.

*Real estate values, especially on property near the
bay, were once very good. Now, however, values have
fallen more than 25 percent.

Conservation Information:

*Some chemical wastes have used up the oxygen in the
water, killing large numbers of fish. Of the 30
species once found in Great Bay, only a few remain.
In the past year, no flounder or mackerel have been
caught at all.

*Of the 140 species of birds previously sighted by
reputable bird watchers, only 30 percent have been
seen in the past year. There is a lack of proper
nesting conditions because the marshlands have been
defoliated as a result of the contamination from
pollution.

*Once clean and inviting, the beaches are now spotted
with dirty sand. Because of poisonous chemical
wastes, the water in the bay has been declared unsafe
for swimming.

the roles

CONSERVA-TIONIST	As a Conservationist, you want to see the proper balance of nature restored in Surfside. Referring to the fact sheet about Surfside and using any other evidence you can think of, you want to argue for Parsons Chemical's Discharge Permit to be rewritten. Now you must prepare your case to present when the Department of Environmental Conservation holds its hearing. (If there is more than one person in your role-group, select a leader.)
MEMBER OF THE DEPARTMENT OF ENVIRONMENTAL CONSERVATION	As a member of the state's Department of Environmental Conservation, you must decide if Parsons Chemical Company's Discharge Permit should be rewritten. Although you think that the protection of Surfside's ecology is of utmost importance, you are realistic enough to know that you should not make a decision that could cause economic disaster in the town. It is up to you to conduct an open, public meeting so that all sides will get a chance to air their views. (If there is more than one person in your role-group, select a leader.) After someone has spoken from each group, you can allow, and also freely participate in, a general discussion of the situation. For the good of the town you want to try to get the entire group to work out a compromise. When the discussion is over, you will have to make your final decision.
TOWN RESIDENT— FACTORY WORKER	As a Factory Worker who lives in Surfside, you depend on Parsons Chemical for your job. If the factory has to reduce operations while installing antipollution devices, you might be out of a job. However, you also see what the pollution is doing to the town: There is a loss of tourist trade income and your own family's leisure-time activities have changed because you can no longer go swimming at the beach or fishing in Great Bay. In preparation for the Department of Environmental Conservation hearing, you want to try to work out a solution that will satisfy all demands to some extent. (If there is more than one person in your role-group, select a leader.)

TOWN RESIDENT—UNEMPLOYED MALE

You are an Unemployed Male who has not worked for four months. You are looking forward to getting a job at Parsons Chemical, but you realize that the pollution problem is serious. You are hoping that a compromise can be worked out so that Parsons will not have to reduce its number of employees while it installs antipollution devices. In preparation for the coming hearing called by the Department of Environmental Conservation, you want to try to work out a solution that will recognize the needs of all the groups concerned. (If there is more than one person in your role-group, select a leader.)

TOWN RESIDENT—RESTAURANT OWNER

As a Restaurant Owner in Surfside, you know that tourists are a large part of your business. Now that they don't come to Surfside very much anymore, your business has fallen off. The pollution of Great Bay has affected your leisure time also, for when there were fish in the bay you used to like to take your children fishing on the day your restaurant was closed. At the same time, however, you realize that if Parsons Chemical lays off workers while it installs an automated waste disposal system, the town's general economy and your business will suffer. In preparation for the Department of Environmental Conservation hearing, you want to try to work out a solution that will deal with the problem. (If there is more than one person in your role-group, select a leader.)

PARSONS CHEMICAL COMPANY EXECUTIVE

As an Executive of Parsons Chemical Company, you want the town to leave you alone. Your chief concern is that you might be forced to turn to an expensive automated waste disposal system. An outside consulting firm has estimated for you that such a system would drastically reduce the amount of pollutants emptied into the bay, but it would cost over 50 percent of the company's profits for a full year. Moreover, the system would take six months to install, during which time you would have to lay off at least half of your workers. You are disturbed by these problems and you feel that if the town is not willing to cooperate with Parsons in some way, you might have to consider moving your business elsewhere. Now you must be ready to argue your position at the hearing called by the Department of Environmental Conservation. (If there is more than one person in your role-group, select a leader.)

communication actions

running a simulation-game

In "Conservation Crisis" each role is taken by, or given to, a different person—or, if possible, group of persons. The idea is to involve as many people as possible. For ease of identification, each person writes his or her role-title on a name tag (blanks available p. 143) and pins it on. Next, the Situation Statement is read aloud by the teacher or a student, and the action is started by all members of each separate role-group getting together to read the rest of the "Conservation Crisis" materials and to plan what they will say at the public hearing called by the Member(s) of the Department of Environmental Conservation. To help communication during the simulation-game, each person can use a Simulation-Game Work Sheet at the back of the book. Next, everyone is called together by the Member(s) of the Department of Environmental Conservation for the public hearing where the participants informally act out what they think would go on at such a meeting. Finally, the role-group responsible for making a decision confers and announces its ruling.

sharpening skills

In addition to running a simulation-game by informally acting out "Conservation Crisis," you can use the materials in the simulation-game as a basis for sharpening your skills in the four areas related to effective communication in English: speaking, listening, reading, and writing.

SPEAKING ACTIONS

1. Take the role of the Conservationist in "Conservation Crisis." Assume that no one in Surfside is concerned about the deteriorating environmental situation, and you have now been given the chance to air your views on a local television community-affairs program. Develop the speech you would give. As you do so, remember that you want to arouse public indignation so that people will come to the aid of the cause of conservation in their town.

2. Suppose that you are a young person (pick an age between 10 and 15) who lives in Surfside, the town described in "Conservation Crisis." Assume that you have been asked to attend the public hearing called by the Department of Environmental Conservation. You have been asked for one reason: to present the point of view of the children of Surfside. Develop the speech you would give. As you

do so, remember that children are affected both by a disruption in recreational facilities and also by an overall attitude toward life and the future expressed by conditions in the town.

3. Suppose that you are a writer and actor who has been asked to develop a one-minute commercial for radio or television to call attention to problems of pollution in the world. Develop the commercial and then deliver it. First, select the subject of your commercial (forest fires, overpopulation, littering, air pollution, or whatever you want to advertise.) Next, decide if your commercial will be for radio or television. Then, try to work up a convincing, dynamic presentation.

4. Does your town or neighborhood have a pollution problem? Assume that you have been asked to make a public service announcement that will be heard on radio and television. Develop the announcement you would make. As you do so, remember that in your announcement you have been asked to present the problem and to suggest ways in which all citizens can help to combat the problem.

5. Be prepared to defend or oppose any one of the following debate topics or statements:
   (a) Man has a right to use, not abuse, of the products of nature.
   (b) Live for today and don't worry about the future.
   (c) "I don't know if there are men on the moon, but if there are they must be using the earth as their lunatic asylum." (George Bernard Shaw)
   (d) "It is always sound business to take an obtainable net gain, at any cost and at any risk to the rest of the community." (Thorstein Veblen)

LISTENING ACTIONS

1. Ask someone who has worked on an antipollution or conservation campaign about how successful it was. (If you do not know anyone who has been active in these causes, ask people you know to assume that they have been.) Listen to the responses you get, not only for factual content but also for impressions the campaigners have of public and political responsiveness to community problems.

2. Ask someone who owns a business whether he or she would be willing to reduce profits for a year or so in order to improve something in the business that is causing pollution. (If you do not know someone who owns a business, ask people you know to assume that they do.) Listen to the responses you get, not only for the specific answer but also for underlying attitudes toward the public and toward money.

3. Take a poll among 15–20 people by asking them if they find that pollution directly affects their lives. As you listen to the responses you get, try to hear not only the factual content but also under-

lying atitudes toward personal involvement, placing of responsibility, and the like. As you take your poll, take brief notes and then see if you can discern patterns in the answers.

4. During a single weekday try to listen for unnecessary noises that create noise pollution in your environment. Keep a record of what you hear and then ask other people if they think the noises on your list are problems. See how many people hear the noises and how many have become resigned to the noises because they assume everyone else has.

READING ACTIONS

SQ3R

Reread "Conservation Crisis," following the SQ3R (Survey, Question, Read, Review, Recite) approach discussed in the Reading section in the chapter on communication skills at the back of this book. The SQ3R approach will make it easier for you to become familiar with all the material in "Conservation Crisis."

Detailed Reading and Reacting

Here are questions that call upon your ability to read for main idea, major details, inferences (getting at underlying attitudes) and then to form your own opinions. Sharp skills in these four reading areas will help you to be an expert reader.

I. *Main Idea*
 A. What is the problem in Surfside?
 B. What is the point of view of each separate role?

II. *Major Details*
 A. The Situation Statement
  1. What was Surfside like before it had a pollution problem?
  2. Why is Parsons Chemical Company a valued part of Surfside?
 B. Fact Sheet About Surfside
  1. What are some of the town's smaller businesses?
  2. What has happened to real estate values in the town?
  3. How many species of fish and of birds were once found around Surfside?
 C. The photographs
  What does each photograph show?
 D. The Roles
  1. According to the Parsons Executive, what are the problems involved in installing antipollution equipment in the factory?
  2. What might Parsons have to do if the town does not cooperate?

III. Inference
A. The Situation Statement
Why is it important to know all of the good things that Parsons Chemical Company does?
B. The Roles
Why does the member of the Department of Environmental Conservation want to work out a compromise?

IV. Opinion
A. What do you think should be done in Surfside?
B. Do you think business considerations should come before leisure-time considerations?

Vocabulary Study

Here are some words you have read in "Conservation Crisis." (They are listed in the order in which they appeared.) Do you know the meaning of each? For a discussion of how to study vocabulary, look at the Reading section of the chapter on communication skills at the back of this book.

conservation . . . conservationist	blue collar
ecological . . . ecology	civil servants
bird sanctuary	real estate
marina	contamination
boat stations	poisonous
pollutants	consulting firm
defoliated	estimated
marshland	drastically
environmental . . . environment	antipollution devices
automated	tourist trade
white collar	leisure-time

Additional Reading

1. Look under "ecology," "conservation," or "pollution" in the card catalog of your college or public library. Take out some books and read about the entire range of problems that exist in modern times.

2. Be on the alert for newspaper and magazine articles and editorials about pollution and conservation. Compare and contrast the problems mentioned with those you read about in "Conservation Crisis."

3. Would you like specific information about pollution and government action in the United States? You can write for a free catalog which will give a complete list of available free materials from: The United States Environmental Protection Agency, Office of Public Affairs, Washington, D.C. 20560.

As a result of taking part in the simulation-game "Conservation Crisis" (or just reading it), you can probably think of many ideas to write about. Below are some suggestions for both paragraph and essay topics. The topics range from those directly related to "Conservation Crisis" to those on the general topic of pollution, conservation, and ecology. For your convenience, any topic that fits into one or more of the rhetorical forms mentioned in the Writing section of the chapter on communication skills at the back of this book is followed by one or more of these symbols in parentheses: D for description; N for narration; Def. for definition; P for process; R for report; and A&P for argument and persuasion.

*Paragraph
Writing*

1. What do you think Parsons Chemical Company should do about its problems? Write a paragraph in which you express and support your opinion.   (A&P)

2. How does pollution affect your recreation activities? Write a paragraph in which you discuss the situation.   (P, N, D)

3. Man is the only animal that kills other animals only for the sport of it. Should this be permitted? Write a paragraph in which you present and support your point of view.   (A&P)

4. Do you think smoking should be permitted in enclosed public areas? Write a paragraph in which you present and support your opinion.   (A&P)

Essay Writing

1. Write a position paper in which you express your opinion about the conservation problem in Surfside. Follow the position paper pattern given in the Writing section of the chapter on communication skills at the back of this book. Assume that your paper will be read by the head of the Department of Environmental Conservation, who was not at the open meeting but who must make the final decision about the Discharge Permit.   (R, A&P)

2. Do you consider yourself personally responsible for any pollution? Write an essay in which you discuss your contributions to pollution —perhaps using the title, "I Am a Polluter."   (N, Def., P)

3. Many people talk about pollution, but not all people agree on exactly what it is. Do you think it has to do with the air and water only, or do you think it relates also to land use and noise levels? Write a definition essay in which you develop your concept of pollution. As you do so, you might want to consider more broad-ranging areas, such as language distortion for advertising and for government information purposes.   (Def.)

4. A famous cartoon character, Pogo, often commented, "We have met the enemy and he is us." In what ways do you think Pogo meant that people are their own worst enemies? Write an essay in which you discuss the various meanings of this statement.   (Def., A&P)

5. Read through the speaking, listening, and opinion reading questions given for "Conservation Crisis." Write an essay on any one of the topics that interests you.

6. If the present rate of pollution were to continue unchecked, what do you think the planet would look like in the year 2000? Write an essay in which you describe either the planet or a smaller area such as your city or your neighborhood. As you do so, remember to try to give the mood and feeling as well as the specific contents of your vision. To make your description as effective as possible, be sure to refer to the five senses (sight, hearing, touch, taste, and smell) as you write. (D)

7. Can people improve on nature? Or do you think that nature should be left alone without any interference? Think about areas such as agriculture, health care, food products, weather control, and so forth. Write an essay in which you discuss your ideas. As you do so, try to consider both the advantages and disadvantages of interference with nature. (A&P)

8. Here are some statements about pollution, ecology, and conservation. Select one statement that interests you and develop an essay around it: (A&P, Def., P)

   (a) Conservation means the wise use of the earth and its resources for the lasting good of man.

   (b) "Man must go back to nature for information." (Thomas Paine)

   (c) "The economic and technological triumphs of the past few years have not solved as many problems as we thought they would, and in fact, have brought us new problems we did not foresee." (Henry Ford II)

women on patrol

a simulation-game for English about the roles of the sexes

the roles

(6 to 35)

REPRESENTATIVE OF THE CHIEF OF POLICE

MALE POLICE OFFICER

FEMALE POLICE OFFICER

WIFE OF A MALE POLICE OFFICER

REPRESENTATIVE OF THE POLICEMEN'S BROTHERHOOD ASSOCIATION

REPRESENTATIVE OF THE FOUNDATION FOR POLICE RESEARCH

the situation

In Newfield, a large American city, the Chief of Police is facing a major confrontation with his male police officers. Last week, in response to a city-wide order from the mayor's office that there be no discrimination on the basis of sex, the Chief commanded that female police officers be assigned to patrol duty just as men are. The male police officers reacted with anger and fear, for they felt that women could not be relied upon to be strong and forceful partners. The female police officers, on the other hand, were happy that the new order would finally give them a chance to participate in more than secretarial police work.

Although the union, called the Policemen's Brotherhood Association, has recently opened its membership to female police officers, it supports the male police officers' position, emphasizing that women might not be able to handle dangerous showdowns on the streets. In addition, the wives of the male police officers are very upset not only because they fear for their husbands' safety, but also because they do not want their husbands working too closely with other women.

In an effort to resolve this highly sensitive problem, the Chief of Police's office has scheduled an open meeting to be attended by representatives of the Chief of Police, the male police officers, the female police officers, the male police officers' wives, the union, and representatives of the Foundation for Police Research. In preparation for this meeting, the Chief of Police requested that the Foundation for Police Research submit a summary report on women in police work. (A copy of the report is given on the next page.) The outcome of the open meeting will unquestionably influence future actions of the Newfield Police Department concerning women on patrol duty.

SUMMARY REPORT FROM THE FOUNDATION FOR POLICE RESEARCH

Background:

Women in police work: For many years in the United States.

Women on patrol duty: Before 1972, only seven known in the United States; by 1974, over 400 in the United States with the number increasing yearly.

Locations Where Women Are Given Police Patrol Duty:

Foreign Countries: Europe (since 1966) and Israel (since 1960).

United States: More than eighty communities, including large cities such as Washington, D.C., San Francisco, and Dallas; and small communities such as Salinas, Kansas and Bogalusa, Louisiana.

Evaluations in United States So Far:

Study of the effectiveness of women on patrol has only begun. The majority of reports are favorable, but based on limited information.

... In Miami, a female police officer arrested one of the F.B.I.'s ten most wanted fugitives.

... In Portland, an observer in the sheriff's office reported that female police officers provoke less violent reactions than do male police officers when the female officers appear, whether to face an unruly crowd or to work out a family argument.

... In St. Louis, a teacher of police reported that female police officers were better at keeping the peace at public housing projects.

... In New York City, a probationary female police officer became so flustered during a violent confrontation that she was unable to radio for assistance, and her driver—a male officer—was roughed up.

... In Washington, D.C., inexperienced female police officers were judged to be less effective than inexperienced male police officers when it came to arrests and traffic violations. Once they gained experience, however, the female police officers had records similar to those of experienced male police officers. It was also observed that female police officers were more likely to take a subordinate role in an incident than were the male police officers. (A three-month study)

... In Cleveland, three nights after a female police officer first went on patrol, she gave chase to one of three holdup men and captured him at gunpoint while her two male colleagues were holding the others against a wall.

the
roles

**REPRESENTATIVE
OF THE
CHIEF OF
POLICE**

You have a problem on your hands! You, along with the Chief of Police, are worried about the discontent in the Newfield Police Department ever since it was announced that female police officers cers would be assigned to patrol duty just as men are. You know that discrimination on the basis of sex is illegal. In addition, the personnel department has experienced some difficulty in recruiting qualified men. Yet you also know that most male police officers just wouldn't feel safe walking the beat or riding in a patrol car with a woman as a partner. It is up to you to conduct an open meeting so that all sides will get a chance to air their views. (If there is more than one person in your role-group, select a leader.) After someone has spoken from each group, you can allow and also freely participate in a general discussion of the problem. Try to get the entire group to work out a possible solution. Then you must make your final recommendations to the Chief of Police, your boss.

**MALE POLICE
OFFICER**

Oh no! You absolutely do not want female police officers to be assigned to patrol duty. They belong in secretarial jobs, at the switchboards, and sometimes at the questioning of female suspects. If you had a female police officer for a partner, what would happen if there were danger? She would probably freeze. Who would help you if you had to handcuff some unruly, husky guys? What would happen if it were necessary to chase on foot a robber or murderer? Women, you feel, are simply not strong or brave enough to do the job of a police officer. It is up to you to present your views—use whatever arguments you can think of, not only the ones given here—at an open meeting called to discuss the problem. (If there is more than one person in your role-group, select a leader.)

FEMALE POLICE OFFICER	At last! Now you are going to have a chance to do the work you've always wanted to do: to help to keep the peace and to make greater contact with the public. You resent the restriction of all female police officers to desk jobs as secretaries, switchboard operators, or—if they are lucky—to the job of questioning female and/or juvenile suspects. You want female police officers to have an equal chance to walk a beat or work in a patrol car. You have had exactly the same training as men, including self-defense, and you feel that women make excellent patrol partners. It is up to you to present your views—use whatever arguments you can think of, not only the ones given here—at an open meeting called to discuss the problem. (If there is more than one person in your role-group, select a leader.)
WIFE OF A MALE POLICE OFFICER	Female police officers on patrol duty? The idea disturbs you very much! You do not feel that your husband will be safe with a female police officer as a partner walking a beat or working in a patrol car. You think that women should not consider themselves the equals of men. Also, you are frankly worried about your husband spending so much of his time with another woman; even if she is working with him. There are enough worries being the wife of a male police officer without having a new worry added. It is up to you to present your views—use whatever arguments you can think of, not only the ones given here—at an open meeting called to discuss the problem. (If there is more than one person in your role-group, select a leader.)
REPRESENTATIVE OF THE FOUNDATION FOR POLICE RESEARCH	More and more research in the past few years has shown that female police officers are highly capable of doing all types of police work, including patroling on foot and in police cars. Your foundation, located in New York City, is a nonprofit group that has been set up to study various problems in all aspects of police work in the United States. You have been asked to attend the open meeting called by the Newfield Chief of Police's office so that you can bring the research information your foundation has gathered. Some of your major recent research findings concerning female police officers are summarized in the written report which you recently submitted to the Chief of Police. It is up to you to give evidence supporting the view that female police officers should be given patrol duty. As you speak at the open meeting, you can refer to your summary report and to whatever other arguments you can think of. (If there is more than one person in your role-group, select a leader.)

(continued)

REPRESENTATIVE OF THE POLICEMEN'S BROTHERHOOD ASSOCIATION

The idea of using women on patrol is out of the question! Ever since your union was established over a hundred years ago, it has fought for the rights and the well-being of the policemen it represents. You feel that equal rights and laws against sex discrimination simply do not apply here. Female police officers should stay at the desk jobs, even if their chances for advancement within the Police Department are limited. Being practical, your union has decided to open its membership to female police officers. You want to keep the girls happy, but you think they should stay in their place and not make trouble. It is up to you to present your views—use whatever arguments you can think of, not only the ones given here—at an open meeting called to discuss the problem. (If there is more than one person in your role-group, select a leader.)

communication actions

running a simulation-game

In "Women on Patrol" each role is taken by, or given to, a different person—or, if possible, group of persons. The idea is to try to involve as many people as possible. For ease of identification, each person writes his or her role-title on a name tag (blanks available p. 143) and pins it on. Next, the Situation Statement is read aloud by the teacher or a student, and the action is started by all members of each separate role-group getting together to read the rest of the "Women on Patrol" materials and to plan what they will say at the open meeting called by the Representative(s) of the Chief of Police. To help communication during the simulation-game, each person can use a Simulation-Game Work Sheet at the back of the book. Next, everyone is called together by the Representative(s) of the Chief of Police for the open meeting where the participants informally act out what they think would go on at such a meeting. Finally, the role-group responsible for making a decision confers and announces its ruling.

sharpening skills

In addition to running a simulation-game by informally acting out "Women On Patrol," you can use the materials in the simulation-game as a basis for sharpening your skills in the four areas related to effective communication in English: speaking, listening, reading, and writing.

SPEAKING ACTIONS

1. Take the role of any of the people in "Women on Patrol." Assume that you have been given a chance to air your views on a local television community-affairs program. Develop the speech you would give. As you do so, remember that your audience might not know anything about the dispute at the Newfield Police Department, so you will have to explain the background of the problem as well as present your opinion on the matter.

2. Suppose that you are a woman who has applied for training as a police officer. Assume that you have passed the written entrance test and now must appear for an interview with a committee of five police admissions officers at the Police Academy. You know that the first question you will be asked is, "Why do you want to become a police officer?" Develop the three- to five-minute informal speech you would give in answer.

3. Suppose that you are the female police officer in the first photograph shown in "Women on Patrol." Prepare a three-to-five-minute monologue of what you might be saying to yourself as you patrol on your motorcycle.

4. Have you ever noticed the image given to women in many situation comedies on television? Suppose that you have been making a study of this and you have now been invited to speak before a group of television writers and program directors. Develop the speech you would give. As you do so, remember to refer to specific programs, specific characters, and—if possible—specific incidents.

5. Be prepared to defend or oppose any one of the following debate topics:
   (a) There should be job discrimination on the basis of sex in certain fields.
   (b) Woman's place is in the home.
   (c) Television ads degrade women.
   (d) Little boys should be brought up differently from girls.

LISTENING ACTIONS

1. Ask a male police officer whether he thinks female police officers should be assigned to walk beats and ride in patrol cars. (If you do not know a male police officer, ask people you know to assume that they are male police officers.) As you listen to the answers you get, try to hear whether his reasons are based on facts or emotions. Also, when he refers to women, listen to his choice of words and see if they reflect his underlying attitudes.

2. Ask the wife of a male police officer how she feels about female police officers being assigned to patrol duty. (If you do not know the wife of a male police officer, ask people you know to assume that they are wives of male police officers.) Compare what you hear with the attitude of the wife of the male police officer in "Women on Patrol." Listen to the responses you get, not only for factual content but also for underlying attitudes toward both sexes and toward the institution of marriage.

3. Take a poll among 15-20 people by asking them if they were in danger they would feel adequately protected if a female police officer came to their aid. As you listen to the answers, try to hear not only the specific answers but also general underlying attitudes about the role and place of women in society. As you take your poll, take brief notes and then see if you can discern patterns in the answers.

4. When you are in the company of a married couple, listen to how they speak to each other. Also, listen to one of the television quiz games, if available, that deals with dating or being newly married, or the like. Try to hear implied attitudes towards men and towards women in general.

Reread "Women on Patrol," following the SQ3R (Survey, Question, Read, Review, Recite) approach discussed in the Reading section in the chapter on communication skills at the back of this book. The SQ3R approach will make it easier for you to become familiar with all the material in "Women on Patrol."

Detailed Reading and Reacting

Here are questions that call upon your ability to read for main idea, major details, inference (getting at underlying attitudes), and then to form your own opinions. Sharp skills in these four reading areas will help you to be an expert reader.

I. *Main Idea*
    A. What is the problem in the Newfield Police Department?
    B. What are the major findings of the Foundation for Police Research?

II. *Major Details*
    A. The Situation Statement
        Why was an open meeting called by the Chief of Police?
    B. Summary Report, Foundation for Police Research
        1. In what foreign countries do female police officers have regular patrol duty?
        2. In Washington, D.C., how do the records of the experienced female police officers compare with those of the experienced male police officers?
    C. The Roles
        According to the Representative of the Policemen's Brotherhood Association, what are the chances for promotion while at a desk job within the police department?

III. *Inference*
    A. The Situation Statement
        Why did the Chief of Police decide to obtain a report from, and invite to the meeting a representative of, the Foundation for Police Research?
    B. Summary Report, Foundation for Police Research
        1. Why might female police officers provoke less violent reactions when they appear at the scene of trouble?
        2. Does the incident in New York City imply that a similar reaction cannot happen to a male police officer?
        3. Why is it important to note that the Washington, D.C. evaluation is based on a three-month study?

IV. *Opinion*
    A. Do you think female police officers should be assigned to patrol duty? Why or why not?
    B. In general, do you tend to trust results of research or your own personal feelings about an issue? Explain.

Here are some words you have read in "Women on Patrol." (They are listed in the order in which they appeared.) Do you know the meaning of each? For a discussion of how to study vocabulary, look at the Reading section of the chapter on communication skills at the back of this book.

confrontation	fugitives	subordinate
discrimination	provoke	colleagues
showdown	unruly	discontent
resolve	probationary	recruiting
sensitive	flustered	resent

Additional Reading

1. Look under "police" in the card catalog of your college or public library. See if there are any books that mention women in police work, and if so, what roles are usually assigned to women?

2. Be on the alert for newspaper and magazine articles and editorials about police work. Are female police officers mentioned at all? If so, what roles are assigned to the women?

WRITING ACTIONS

As a result of taking part in the simulation-game "Women on Patrol" (or just reading it), you can probably think of many ideas to write about. Below are some suggestions for both paragraph and essay topics. The topics range from those directly related to "Women on Patrol" to those on the general topics of women's roles in society and police work. For your convenience, any topic that fits into one or more of the rhetorical forms mentioned in the Writing section of the chapter on communication skills at the back of this book is followed by one or more of these symbols in parentheses: D for description; N for narration; Def. for definition; P for process; R for report; and A&P for argument and persuasion.

Paragraph Writing

1. Do you agree with the point of view of the Male Police Officer in "Women on Patrol"? Write a paragraph in which you express and support your opinion. (A&P)

2. Do you think that assigning female police officers to patrol duty will increase the incidence of married male police officers being unfaithful to their wives? Write a paragraph in which you state and support your opinion. (A&P)

3. Do you think that women are treated as second-class citizens? Write a paragraph in which you present and support your opinion. (A&P, Def., or P)

4. Write a paragraph in which you comment on this quote: "A woman's name should appear in print but twice—when she marries and when she dies." (By various men of the Old South) (A&P)

Essay Writing   1. Write a position paper in which you express your opinion about the confrontation in the Newfield Police Department. Follow the position paper pattern given in the Writing section of the chapter on communication skills at the back of this book. Assume that your paper will be read by the mayor of Newfield who is eager to work out a compromise. (R, A&P)

2. What do you think a police officer should be like? Write an essay in which you define not only the ideal personality and disposition for a police officer but also what you see as a police officer's role in society. (Def.)

3. What makes someone decide that he or she wants to be a police officer? Is the pay attractive or is the idea of helping society the motivation? Is it a family tradition or is it the result of a particular experience in childhood? Write a narrative essay in which you make up the story of someone's life and show how it led to the choice of police work as a career. (N)

4. Read through the speaking, listening, and reading questions given for "Women on Patrol." Write an essay on any one of the topics that interests you.

5. The police department in every community is trying to do its job. Is the one in your community succeeding? Write an essay in which you discuss the police department in your community. What is it doing that is good and how could it become more effective? Try to draw on specific examples so that your statements will be backed up with more than generalizations. (P, A&P)

6. What is your opinion of the Women's Liberation Movement? Write an essay in which you state your point of view. (A&P)

7. Do you remember any childhood experiences that clearly trained you for your sex-role in society? Write an essay in which you recount those experiences, and then evaluate them. Would you want to give your children similar experiences? Explain. (N, A&P)

8. Here are some statements and questions about the sexes. Select one statement that interests you and develop an essay around it: (A&P, Def., or P)
    (a) Most men are male chauvinists.
    (b) Are women inferior to men?
    (c) "There is nothing enduring in life for a woman except what she builds in a man's heart." (Judith Anderson)
    (d) "What are little boys made of? Snips and snails, and puppy dogs' tails; . . . What are little girls made of? Sugar and spice and everything nice." (Nursery Rhyme)

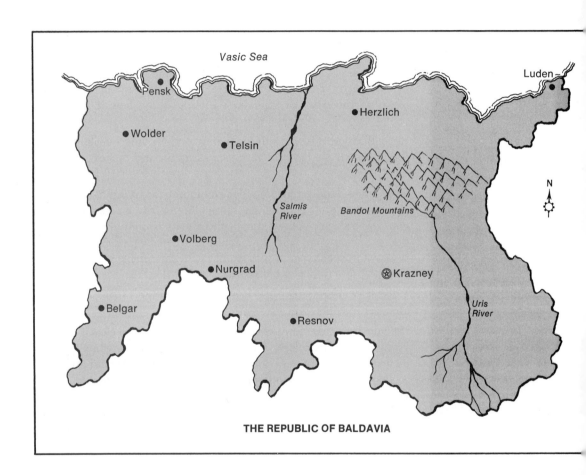

THE REPUBLIC OF BALDAVIA

dollars in demand

the roles

(6 to 36)

DEFENSE MINISTRY OFFICIAL

HEALTH MINISTRY OFFICIAL

TRANSPORTATION MINISTRY OFFICIAL

EDUCATION MINISTRY OFFICIAL

ENERGY MINISTRY OFFICIAL

SENATE BUDGET COMMITTEE MEMBER

a simulation-game for English about juggling the government dollar

the
situation

Baldavia, a large fictitious Western Europe republic, is faced with pressing financial problems. These problems are of grave concern to the various Baldavian government Ministries, the departments responsible for the functioning of Baldavian society. The Baldavian Senate is now holding budget hearings, and each Ministry is pressing for money allotments that will relieve immediate as well as long-range difficulties. True, the publicity that Baldavia puts out describes an ideal republic, but the Senate and Ministries know that there is always a wide difference between publicity and reality.

**GRAPHIC SUMMARY OF ALLOTMENT REQUESTS
AND AVAILABLE MONEY
prepared for the Senate Budget Committee: the Republic of Baldavia**

THE GOVERNMENT DOLLAR
for the current fiscal year

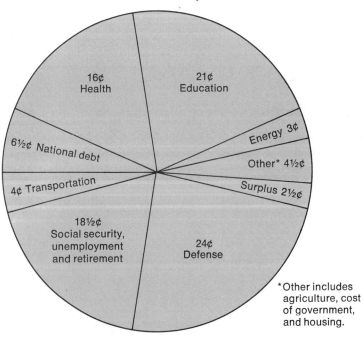

16¢
Health

21¢
Education

Energy 3¢

Other* 4½¢

6½¢ National debt

4¢ Transportation

Surplus 2½¢

18½¢
Social security,
unemployment
and retirement

24¢
Defense

*Other includes
agriculture, cost
of government,
and housing.

The Senate knows that it cannot alleviate the situation by raising taxes because, according to Baldavian law, taxes cannot be increased for the coming year—a reasonable law because Baldavians are already among the most highly taxed people in the world. In its first move toward establishing next year's budget, the Senate at last week's hearing set a final allotment, that cannot be changed, of 29½ percent of Baldavia's revenues for a combination of agriculture, costs of operating the government, housing, the national debt (the interest and principal on money borrowed by the republic), retirement, social security, and unemployment.

At today's final session of the Senate's budget hearings, decisions will be made about the rest of next year's allotments for the extremely important areas of defense, education, energy, health, and transportation. (A graphic summary of requests and available money is given on the following page.) Without a doubt, decisions made at today's hearings will deeply affect Baldavia's future stability.

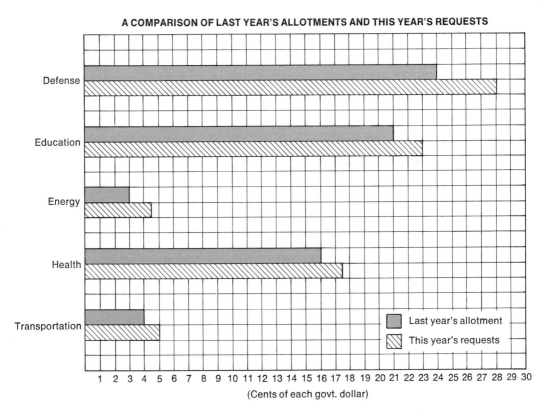

A COMPARISON OF LAST YEAR'S ALLOTMENTS AND THIS YEAR'S REQUESTS

Defense

Education

Energy

Health

Transportation

Last year's allotment

This year's requests

1 2 3 4 5 6 7 8 9 10 11 12 13 14 15 16 17 18 19 20 21 22 23 24 25 26 27 28 29 30

(Cents of each govt. dollar)

For decision of Senate Budget Committee:

Defense wants	.28¢
Education wants	.23¢
Energy wants	.04½ ¢
Health wants	.17½ ¢
Transportation wants	.05¢
Already Allotted by Senate Budget Committee	.29½ ¢

(final, cannot be changed)

TOTAL NEEDS FOR NEXT YEAR	$1.07½

Money available:

Total for each government dollar from next year's receipts	$1.00
Surplus from this year	.02½ ¢
TOTAL AVAILABLE MONEY FOR NEXT YEAR	−$1.02½

AMOUNT OF MONEY SHORTAGE FOR NEXT YEAR	.05 ¢

Total requests exceed available money by .05¢; compromises will have to be made

Author's Note: We recognize that in reality national appropriations are requested and filled in terms of actual dollars, not cents of the government dollar. However, because an industrialized country as Baldavia with 55,000,000 people could conceivably have a budget that runs into the tens of billions of dollars, we felt that if we were to use real budget terms, the numbers would overwhelm our prime purpose in designing this simulation-game. Our intention is to provoke assessment of values and priorities; we decided, therefore, to simplify the monetary aspect of the situation by working in terms of cents on the dollar.

THE PLIGHT OF BALDAVIA

BALDAVIA AT A GLANCE
a guide for the visitor

It is worth getting to know the Republic of Baldavia. Not only is she one of the countries in the heart of Europe that people like to visit, but she is at the same time a modern state and a leading industrial nation. In Baldavia the old joins with the new, the past with the present. Seven hundred years have left their mark on this country.

Baldavia's special characteristic is her great diversity. What is "typically Baldavian" has always been a subject of controversy. Baldavia—does that mean the old citadels and castles, the romantic Salmis River, the ancient, sleepy little towns? Or does anyone who says Baldavia mean her modern technology and industry, cars, and atomic power plants that support a nation of 55,000,000 people? As one travels across Baldavia's 208,000 square miles (approximately the same size as France or Spain), it becomes apparent that Baldavia is all this—and more.

DEFENSE

Always mindful of her role as a world power, Baldavia maintains a peace-keeping force of 285,000 men equipped with the most up-to-date armaments: guided missiles, guided missile cruisers, American amphibious armored vehicles, and advanced fighter airplanes. In addition to ensuing internal security, the Baldavian army, navy, and air force help to check the spread of Communism in Western Europe. As a member of the North Atlantic Treaty Organization (NATO), Baldavia is committed to defending the sea, air and land routes of her neighboring countries. In addition, Baldavia's armed forces are available to perform duties within the framework of United Nations peace-keeping operations.

EDUCATION

Long known for her fine system of education, Baldavia takes pride in the network of state-supported nursery, primary, intermediate and secondary schools that serve over 7,000,000 students. Although Baldavians are required to attend school only until they reach 16 years of age, over half of all secondary school graduates continue their education at a college, university, or vocational center. The Baldavian government provides subsidies for these institutions of higher education and also offers scholarships for selected students who cannot afford tuition costs.

ENERGY

To keep pace with the ever-growing demand for energy, Baldavia is in the process of developing a host of new power sources. At the foot of the majestic Bandol Mountains, oil companies are mining shale, a mineral rock that when heated actually "bleeds" oil. In the suburbs of Krazney, the national capital, Baldavia's first atomic power plant is being constructed at a cost of over $600,000,-000. Throughout the Wolder Valley region, government engineers are drilling mile-deep wells that will tap underground fields of dry steam. Atomic power and dry-steam power are expected to be more economical and efficient than oil and coal power.

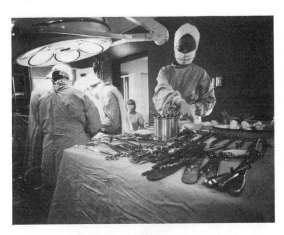

HEALTH

Reflecting Baldavia's spirit of social welfare, the National Health Plan guarantees medical and psychiatric care to all citizens. Most health services are provided at government supported hospital clinics staffed by well-trained doctors and nurses. Although the patient must pay a small fee of 50¢ for each clinic visit and $1.00 for each day of hospitalization, the plan is financed primarily through a special tax on employees and employers. Socialized medicine is just one way in which the Baldavian government meets its obligation to its people.

TRANSPORTATION

Baldavians are a people on the go! The nation's highways are crowded with over 14,000,000 cars, double the number of cars just ten years ago. To meet its citizens' travel needs, the Baldavian government runs a national railway system from border to border. Under a government grant, the city of Pensk is now constructing a monorail that will provide fast and efficient train service from the suburbs to the downtown business district. In addition, airports are situated in many of the republic's major cities, making Baldavia the gateway country of Western Europe.

Published by the Government Press and Information Office of the Republic of Baldavia, Krazney, 1975

the
roles

DEFENSE MINISTRY OFFICIAL

As a Baldavian Defense Ministry Official, you have had major problems during the last year. Soldiers are complaining vigorously about poor working and living conditions, so there has been a sharp decline in enlistments. Also, Russia has continued to experiment with intercontinental ballistic missiles and other advanced weapons, while much of the Baldavian military equipment is becoming outdated. It is up to you to persuade the Senate Budget Committee to increase your funds from 24¢ to 28¢ per government dollar so that you can deal with these problems. (If there is more than one person in your role-group, select a leader.)

HEALTH MINISTRY OFFICIAL

As a Health Ministry Official, you have witnessed a year of turmoil in the public health system. The doctors at the hospital clinic have been complaining about the lack of staff and equipment to provide proper medical and psychiatric care. Moreover, many doctors have threatened to quit and go into private practice if their salaries are not raised. At the same time, many patients have been complaining about having to wait for hours to see a doctor and for weeks to get a hospital bed. It is up to you to persuade the Senate Budget Committee to increase your funds from 16¢ to 17½¢ per government dollar so that you can deal with these problems. (If there is more than one person in your role-group, select a leader.)

TRANSPORTATION MINISTRY OFFICIAL

As a Transportation Ministry Official, your biggest concern at the moment is to settle the strike by the Baldavian Brotherhood of Railway Employees over their salary demands and working conditions. Furthermore, you are aware that Baldavia's mass transit system is undependable and uncomfortable. If the transit facilities were improved, people would be encouraged to leave their cars at home, thereby saving significant amounts of gasoline and reducing traffic congestion and air pollution in the large cities. It is up to you to persuade the Senate Budget Committee to increase your funds from 4¢ to 5¢ per government dollar so that you can deal with these problems. (If there is more than one person in your role-group, select a leader.)

EDUCATION MINISTRY OFFICIAL

As a Baldavian Education Ministry Official, you have been subjected to a great many pressures during the last year. Parent complaints that the entire school system is overcrowded and understaffed are not unusual, but recently these complaints grew much worse when it was announced that over half the republic's schoolchildren are reading below grade level. Also, because overcrowding has been a major problem in Baldavia's medical schools, a shortage of doctors now exists in the hospital clinics. To add to these problems, the latest college census figures indicate that because of limited scholarship funds only a very small percentage of students from low income areas are able to attend a higher education institution. It is up to you to persuade the Senate Budget Committee to increase your funds from 21¢ to 23¢ per government dollar to help you deal with these problems. (If there is more than one person in your role-group, select a leader.)

ENERGY MINISTRY OFFICIAL

As an Energy Ministry Official you are deeply disturbed by Baldavia's energy crisis. People have responded to electricity brownouts and gasoline shortages by buying fewer cars and major appliances, and by taking fewer car trips to Baldavia's resort areas. In addition, because of the short supply of petrochemicals, the availability of phonograph records, plastic toys, and nylon and rayon fabrics has sharply decreased. These cutbacks are good for energy conservation, but they are terrible for business and industry. Unemployment is increasing daily. Unless you get additional funds, you will not be able to accelerate the development of new power sources. It is up to you to persuade the Senate Budget Committee to increase your funds from 3¢ to 4½¢ per government dollar to help you deal with these problems. (If there is more than one person in your role-group, select a leader.)

SENATE BUDGET COMMITTEE MEMBER

As a Senate Budget Committee Member, you must devise a national budget for the coming year. Today you must conduct hearings and listen to the money allotment requests made by the Ministries of Defense, Education, Health, and Transportation. After someone from each Ministry has spoken, you can allow, and also freely participate in, a general discussion. A key problem you face is that the total requests exceed available money by 5¢ on the government dollar—even when last year's surplus is used. (Keep in mind that you have already made final allotments to agriculture, government operating costs, housing, the national debt, retirement, social security, and unemployment—for a combined total of 29½¢ of the government dollar that cannot be changed.) Compromises will have to be made. Try to get the entire group to work out a possible solution; then make your final budget recommendations. (If there is more than one person in your role-group, select a leader.)

communication
actions

running a simulation-game

In "Dollars in Demand" each role is taken by, or given to, a different person—or, if possible, group of persons. The idea is to involve as many people as possible. For ease of identification, each person writes his or her role-title on a name tag (blanks available p. 143) and pins it on. Next, the Situation Statement is read aloud by the teacher or a student, and the action is started by all members of each separate role-group getting together to read the rest of the "Dollars in Demand" materials and to plan what they will say at the budget hearings called by the Senate Budget Committee Member(s). To help communication during the simulation-game, each person can use a Simulation-Game Work Sheet at the back of the book. Next, everyone is called together by the Senate Budget Committee Member(s) for the budget hearings where the participants informally act out what they think would go on at such a meeting. Finally, the role-group responsible for making a decision confers and announces its ruling.

sharpening skills

In addition to running a simulation-game by informally acting out "Dollars In Demand," you can use the materials in the simulation-game as a basis for sharpening your skills in the four areas related to effective communication in English: speaking, listening, reading, and writing.

SPEAKING ACTIONS

1. Take the role of the Senate Budget Committee Member in "Dollars In Demand." Assume that you have been given a chance to air your views on a local television community-affairs program. Develop the speech you would give. As you do so, remember that the television viewers might not realize the seriousness of the republic's budget crisis, so you will have to explain the background of the problem as well as present your opinion on the matter.

2. Suppose that you have applied for an appointment as a government minister in Baldavia. Assume that you have already had several preliminary interviews with varous government officials and now you must appear for an interview with the President of the Republic. You know that the first question the President will ask is, "Which Ministry would you want to work for and why?" Develop the three-to-five-minute informal speech you would give in answer.

3. In Baldavia, as in many countries, conservationists are complaining that the land is being destroyed to provide sources of energy. Companies involved in coal and shale mining and in the construction of cross-country oil pipelines insist that these methods are necessary if the nation's energy supplies are to be maintained. Assume that you have been invited to speak at a government hearing about this problem. Develop the speech you would give. As you do so, remember to support your opinions with solid evidence.

4. Be prepared to defend or oppose any one of the following debate topics:
   (a) Medical care in America should be free.
   (b) "Education is a better safeguard of liberty than a standing army." (Edward Everett)
   (c) "Politics is the conduct of public affairs for private advantage." (Ambrose Bierce)

LISTENING ACTIONS

1. Listen to a radio or television interview of a politician. What are the major problems he discusses? What solutions does he propose? Compare what you hear with what you have read about Baldavia. Listen to the interview, not only for factual content but also for underlying attitudes, especially as expressed by "loaded language."

2. Ask someone who works for either the federal or state government about the government's effectiveness and efficiency in providing public services. (If you do not know a government worker, ask people you know to assume that they are government workers.) Listen to the responses you get, and try to hear if opinions are based on facts or emotions.

3. Take a poll among 15–20 people by asking them to state this country's most serious problem at the present time. As you listen to the answers, try to hear not only the specific answers but also general underlying attitudes about government and politics. As you take your poll, take brief notes and then see if you can discern patterns in the answers.

4. Listen to a few television newscasts of at least a half hour in length. What national problems are discussed? Compare what you hear with what you have read about Baldavia.

READING ACTIONS

SQ3R

Reread "Dollars in Demand," following the SQ3R (Survey, Question, Read, Review, Recite) approach discussed in the Reading section in the chapter on communication skills at the back of this book. The SQ3R approach will make it much easier for you to become familiar with all the material in "Dollars in Demand."

Here are questions that call upon your ability to read for main idea, major details, inferences (getting at underlying attitudes), and then to form your own opinions. Sharp skills in these four reading areas will help you to be an expert reader.

I. **Main Idea**
   A. What are the basic problems in Baldavia?
   B. What is you general impression of Baldavia as it is described in "Baldavia at a Glance"?

II. **Major Details**
   A. The Situation Statement
      1. Why can't the Senate alleviate the situation by raising taxes?
      2. What budget decisions were made at last week's hearing?
   B. The Baldavian Budget Summary
      1. According to the pie graph, last year how many cents of each government dollar were spent for education? . . . health? . . . defense? . . . energy? . . . transportation? . . . the national debt? . . . social security, unemployment, and retirement?
      2. According to the bar graph, what are the increases in allotment requests for defense? . . . education? . . . energy? . . . health? . . . transportation?
      3. According to the chart of The Arithmetic of the Money Requests and Available Funds Next Year, the total requests exceed available money by how much?
   C. "Baldavia at a Glance"
      1. What percentage of secondary school graduates continues on for further education?
      2. What power sources are being developed in Baldavia?
      3. What does the National Health Plan guarantee?
   D. The Roles
      What are the major problems faced by the officials of each of the ministries?

III. **Inference**
   A. The Situation Statement
      Why is there always a wide difference between a nation's publicity and reality?
   B. The Roles
      1. Why should the Defense Ministry officials be worried about Russia's experimentation with advanced weapons?
      2. Why has Baldavia's energy crisis caused a sharp increase in unemployment?
   C. Baldavia at a Glance
      If something is published by a country's press and information office, can the content be considered totally objective?

IV. *Opinion*

How many cents of the government dollar should be allocated for defense? . . . education? . . . energy? . . . health? . . . transportation? Remember that 29½¢ of the government dollar has already been set aside for "Other."

Vocabulary Study

Here are some words you have read in "Dollars In Demand." (They are listed in the order in which they appeared.) Do you know the meaning of each? For a discussion of how to study vocabulary, look at the Reading section of the chapter on communication skills at the back of this book.

republic	stability	vigorously
grave	diversity	enlistments
allotments	controversy	census
relieve	citadels	petrochemicals
alleviate	armaments	accelerate
revenues	amphibious	turmoil
debt	vocational	congestion
principal	subsidies	
graphic	majestic	

Additional Reading

1. Look under "defense," "education," "energy," "health," "transportation," or "government and politics" in the card catalog of your college or public library. Also look for these topics as they are listed under the general catalog heading of "United States" or any other country. Take out some books and compare what you read with what you have read about Baldavia.

2. Be on the alert for newspaper and magazine articles and editorials about government budget problems. Compare and contrast the problems mentioned with those you read about in "Dollars In Demand."

WRITING ACTIONS

As a result of taking part in the simulation-game "Dollars In Demand" (or just reading it), you can probably think of many ideas to write about. Below are some suggestions for both paragraph and essay topics. The topics range from those directly related to "Dollars In Demand" to those on the general topics of government, defense, education, energy, health, and transportation. For your convenience, any topic that fits into one or more of the rhetorical forms mentioned in the Writing section of the chapter on communication skills at the back of this book is followed by one or more of these symbols in parentheses: D for description; N for narration; Def. for definition; P for process; R for report; and A&P for argument and persuasion.

Paragraph Writing	1.	How would you solve Baldavia's budget problems? Write a paragraph in which you present your solution. (A&P, P)
	2.	Do you think that a non-Communist country needs to have advanced military weapons like those used by Russia? Write a paragraph in which you present and support your opinion. (A&P)
	3.	Do you think that medical research should be supported by the government or by private foundations? Write a paragraph in which you present and support your opinion. (A&P)
	4.	Should bridge, tunnel, and highway tolls be used to subsidize mass transit fares? Write a paragraph in which you present and support your opinion. (A&P)
	5.	Write a paragraph in which you comment on this quote: "Education is an admirable thing but nothing worth knowing can be taught." (Oscar Wilde) (A&P)
Essay Writing	1.	Write a position paper in which you express your opinion about the budget problems in Baldavia. Follow the position paper pattern given in the Writing section of the chapter on communication skills at the back of this book. Assume that your paper will be read by the prime minister of Baldavia, who was not at the hearing but who must make final recommendations about the budget. (R, A&P)
	2.	What do you think should be a government's responsibilities to its citizens? Write an essay in which you discuss your ideas on this subject. Some of the questions you might want to consider are: Does the government have an obligation to guarantee each person a minimum income? . . . free medical care? . . . free higher education? If so, where should the money come from to pay for these government services? (Def., A&P)
	3.	How can the average person help to conserve energy? Write an essay in which you offer advice on this subject. As you do so, consider not only your car and home but also public uses of energy for transportation, industry, and the like. (P)
	4.	Is your neighborhood overlooked by tourists? Write a publicity brochure that makes your neighborhood seem attractive and interesting to visitors. You might want to include descriptions of its physical appearance as well as of its recreation, education, and transportation facilities. To make your description as effective as possible, be sure to refer to the five senses (sight, hearing, touch, taste, and smell) as you write. (D)
	5.	How can your neighborhood be improved? Write an essay in which you discuss the major problems in your neighborhood. Some of the areas you might want to consider are: housing,

streets, schools, recreation, transportation, and crime. As you do so, try to suggest possible remedies for the problems discussed. (D, A&P)

6. Is the public welfare system an unnecessary burden on the tax-payer? Write an essay in which you discuss your opinion. Some of the questions you might want to consider are: Does the average American have a moral obligation to help those who cannot support themselves? Who should pay for welfare—the city, state, or federal government? What can be done to improve the present welfare system? (A&P, P)

7. Should a powerful nation act as peace-keeper of the world? Write an essay in which you discuss your point of view. Some questions you might want to consider are: Does a powerful nation have a moral obligation to provide military protection for weak countries? Will such protection help the powerful nation to protect itself as well? For a powerful nation, is restraint often more effective than aggression? What limitations, if any, should the nation place on its military involvement in other countries? (A&P)

8. What makes someone decide that he or she wants to be a politician? Is the person motivated by the need for public recognition or the desire to help society? Is the person influenced by family tradition or a particular childhood experience? Write a narrative essay in which you make up the story of someone's life and show how it led to the choice of politics as a career. (N)

9. Read through the speaking, listening, and reading questions given for "Dollars In Demand." Write an essay on any one of the topics that interests you.

10. Here are some statements about government and its services. Select one statement that interests you and develop an essay around it. (A&P, P, Def.)
   (a) "We often say how impressive power is. But I do not find it impressive at all. The guns and the bombs, the rockets and the warships, are all symbols of human failure. They are necessary symbols. They protect what we cherish. But they are witness to human folly." (Lyndon B. Johnson)
   (b) "You can't run a government solely on a business basis . . . Government should be human. It should have a heart." (Herbert H. Lehman)
   (c) "I firmly believe that if the whole *materia medica* [medical knowledge] could be sunk to the bottom of the sea, it would be all the better for mankind, and all the worse for the fishes." (Oliver Wendell Holmes)

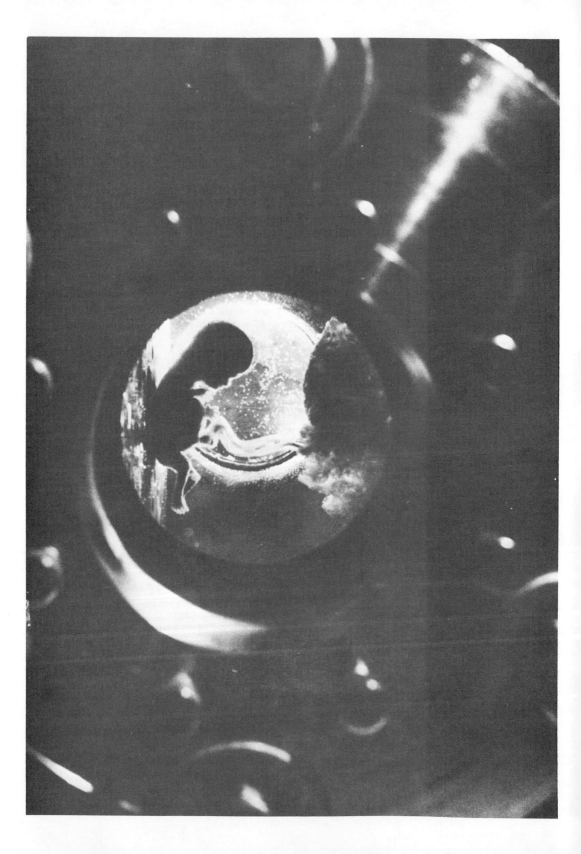

population control 2204

a simulation-game for English about the family of the future

the roles
(6 to 36)

**POPULATION CONTROL
BOARD MEMBER**

**FAMILY UNIT A MEMBER—
AND WITNESS, IF AVAILABLE**

**FAMILY UNIT B MEMBER—
AND WITNESS, IF AVAILABLE**

**FAMILY UNIT C MEMBER—
AND WITNESS, IF AVAILABLE**

**FAMILY UNIT D MEMBER—
AND WITNESS, IF AVAILABLE**

**FAMILY UNIT E MEMBER—
AND WITNESS, IF AVAILABLE**

A view of a densely populated area, 1970's, before population control was instituted.

the
situation

In a few days it will be A.D. 2204 and, as is always the case at the
new year, the Population Control Board of each local neighborhood
must prepare to publish the list of people who have been awarded
Population Growth Permits for the coming year. The Population
Control Board of local neighborhood TN3, one of a vast network of
local neighborhoods in the United States, wants to award as many
Population Growth Permits as possible because it knows how much
some people want to have children. The Population Control Board,
however, is bound by international agreement to award only as many
Population Growth Permits as are permitted by the planet's Central
Population Control Agency. For A.D. 2204, the board has been
authorized to award only three permits.

The Central Population Control Agency was set up over 150 years
ago when the planet reorganized itself to back away from the edge
of disaster that gross overpopulation of the planet had caused. The
planet had simply run out of space, food, and life-sustaining natural
resources. Under the current law, therefore, contraception is compul-
sory for anyone without a Population Growth Permit. If anyone has
a baby illegally, the Population Control Board must declare the
parents forever ineligible for a Population Growth Permit and must
take away the illegal baby and award it to someone who has properly
applied for a baby.

Before deciding which of five sets of applicants are best fit and
motivated to be awarded the three Population Growth Permits
available for the year of 2204, the Population Control Board of local
neighborhood TN3 must conduct an open session of interviews so that
all applicants, and their witnesses if present, can plead in person before
the board. In preparation for this session, all participants have
familiarized themselves with the "Important Communication" memo
sent by the planet's Central Population Control Agency and the
related information given in the "Population Control Manual." (Both
items are given on the following pages.) The outcomes of this meeting
will undoubtedly affect not only the happiness of five family units
but also the future welfare of three children.

IMPORTANT COMMUNICATION   December 1, 2203

    To: Local Neighborhood TN3, Population Control
            Board

    From: Central Population Agency, Earth

    Re: Allotment of Population Growth Permits for
            A.D. 2204

It is hereby decreed that your neighborhood can allot Population Growth Permits for the year 2204 as
follows:

Permit #1   Method: Natural conception*
code TN3 01 2204   (if no male or sterile
                                  male, artificial in-
                                  semination*)

                       Prenatal: Usual care and Decom-
                                  pression Therapy* for
                                  the mother during the
                                  last stages of preg-
                                  nancy
_____

Permit #2   Method: Natural conception*
code TN3 02 2204   (if no male or sterile
                                  male, artificial insem-
                                  ination)

                       Prenatal: Usual care and no Inter-
                                  ference Therapy*
_____

Permit #3   Method: Cloning*
code TN3 07 2203
                       Prenatal: Laboratory grown

                       Special: ADOPTION. Baby was
                                  cloned during 2203 from
                                  its father, a world-
                                  famous concert violinist;
                                  parents died last month in
                                  an accident; baby, a male,
                                  is now three months old.
_____

* For complete definitions of all terms, see "Definitions Section" of the Population Growth Manual.

POPULATION CONTROL MANUAL

DEFINITIONS SECTION (alphabetically listed)

Although many of the processes described below are widely used, they are under the strict control of the Central Population Control Agency because planning of quality is as important as planning of quantity.

Artificial insemination: *Through artificial insemination, a female is impregnated by the artificial introduction of semen. This method, which contrasts to natural insemination achieved through sexual intercourse, calls for injecting sperm cells into a female's uterus during ovulation. Soon after this process was perfected in 1937, sperm banks were established for the temporary storing of sperm cells. In the last hundred years, a new freezing technique has made it possible to store sperm cells undamaged for an indefinite period of time. As a result, the sperm cells of many important men, such as valuable scientists, statesmen, and artists, have been preserved.*

Cloning: *A clone is a descendant of one individual rather than two. A clone is a carbon copy of its parent. Cloning is a scientific process based on the discovery that each cell of a living thing, plant and animal, contains all the information necessary to create a complete copy of that original living thing. This process was first used in England and the United States in the late 1960's for the nonsexual reproduction of some vegetables and lower forms of animals such as frogs. The process was perfected for use on humans about fifty years later. To be cloned, therefore, is to be derived nonsexually from a single cell of one individual; the child that results from this process will grow to be an exact copy of its parent.*

Decompression therapy: *A form of interference therapy, decompression therapy consists of enclosing the abdomen and pelvis of a pregnant woman in a plastic dome in which the atmospheric pressure has been reduced to one-fifth the regular atmospheric pressure. This treatment, given for about thirty minutes a day during the last two weeks of pregnancy, increases the oxygen supply to the fetus (unborn child). Babies born after decompression therapy are superintelligent, and are able to carry on adult conversations at eighteen months, to know many languages at four years, and to engage in advanced abstract thinking as adults. The process of decompression therapy has changed little since it was accidentally discovered in the late 1960's by a South African doctor who was searching for a way to reduce the pains of childbirth. Soon after the process was discovered, it was outlawed because in the Twentieth Century interference with unborn children was illegal.*

Natural conception: *Generally, the term natural conception refers to female impregnation achieved through sexual intercourse. This method of impregnation is in contrast to artificial insemination (defined above) and is, therefore, sometimes referred to as natural insemination.*

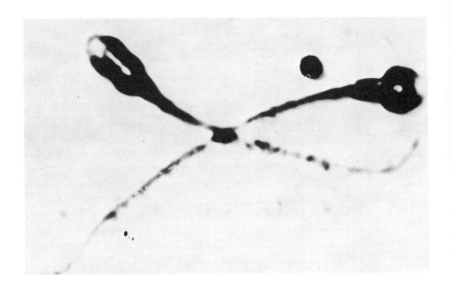

Comparison of male and female sperm.

Interference therapy: *Any kind of treatment that interferes with the natural, random determination of a child's characteristics is referred to as interference therapy. Decompression therapy, sex determination, and test-tube breeding, all defined in this Manual, are specific types of interference therapy.*

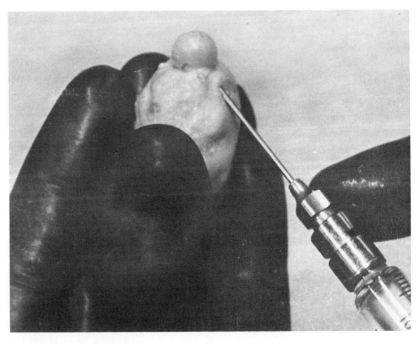

Extracting egg from ovary.

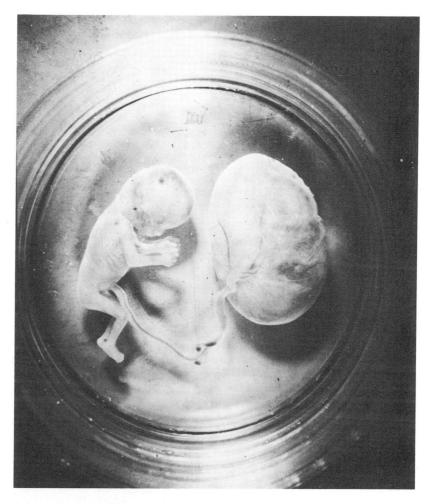

A nine-week-old human embryo in laboratory petri dish.

Sex determination: Because it is the male sperm, not the female egg, that determines the sex of a child, sex determination is a process applied to semen. The semen is filtered so that only male-producing or only female-producing sperm cells remain. By the use of artificial insemination (defined above), the filtered semen is then introduced into the woman. This filtering method, developed in Germany in 1973, was perfected for use with human beings about forty years later.

Test-tube breeding: As a fertilized female egg develops from an embryo (the first three months) to a fetus (the last six months), the egg is freed from the confines of the mother's womb and is then grown in an artificial environment. Since the volume of the human brain, averaging about 1500 milliliters, is determined in a large part by the size of the female pelvis, a child bred in a very large, specially formed test tube develops a brain that is much larger than average. This method of test-tube breeding, although imagined as long as 250 years ago, was perfected only recently and is not yet being used to any great extent.

the roles

**POPULATION
CONTROL
BOARD
MEMBER**

You must select from among five sets of applicants those who deserve to receive one of the three Population Growth Permits you are authorized to distribute for the year 2204. Each set of applicants, together with their witnesses if available, will plea before you in person. You must allow a limited amount of time for each set of applicants and their witnesses to speak. After you have heard from each set, you can open the floor to general discussion during which time you will probably want to ask questions that will help you to make decisions. You will likely not only be interested in the applicants' stated characteristics such as age and occupation but also in such intangible factors as emotional stability, personality, compassion, and desire for children. (If there is more than one person in your role-group, select a leader.) When the discussion is over, you will have to make your final decisions about the allotment of the permits.

**FAMILY UNIT
MEMBERS**

As a Member of one of the Family Units described in the chart on the next page, you want to have a baby very much. You feel that you could provide the care and love needed to raise a child properly, and, in turn, you look forward to the affection and joy that a child can give. Thus, your Family Unit is making application for a Population Growth Permit for the year 2204. But a permit is not easy to get. You are one of five Family Units that will be interviewed by the Population Control Board, which has only three permits to distribute for the year. At your interview, you should first state which specific permit you want. (See "Important Communication" memo for a list of available permits.) Or you may ask for any permit that the board will give you. Keeping in mind that not all applicants can be granted a permit, you will then want to argue that your Family Unit deserves one. After you have addressed the Population Control Board, you may ask your witnesses, if any, to speak on your behalf. (If more than one Member of your Family Unit is present at the interview session, select a leader.)

You are a good friend of one of the Family Units listed on the chart of Population Growth Permit Applicants. Because you have known the members of the Family Unit for a long time, you are aware of their many outstanding qualities. Convinced that the Family Unit would make fine, loving parents, you are happy to speak to the Population Control Board on their behalf. After your friends have made their request to the board, you will have the opportunity to present additional evidence to prove that they deserve a permit. (If there is more than one Witness for your Family Unit, select a leader.)

POPULATION GROWTH PERMIT APPLICANTS

Person	Age	Education	I.Q.	Health	Occupation	Special Comments

FAMILY UNIT A

2 people, one male and one female, married for two years

Person	Age	Education	I.Q.	Health	Occupation	Special Comments
male	27	high school dropout	90	good	hospital orderly	none
female	24	high school dropout	110	good	file clerk	none

FAMILY UNIT B

2 people, one male and one female, married for one year

Person	Age	Education	I.Q.	Health	Occupation	Special Comments
male	32	Ph.D. in English	150	history of ulcers, otherwise good	college professor	married twice before
female	28	college graduate	115	blind, but otherwise good	homemaker	none

FAMILY UNIT C

2 people, two females, together (not married) for five years

Person	Age	Education	I.Q.	Health	Occupation	Special Comments
female	34	high school graduate	110	good	interior decorator	none
female	48	Ph.D.	160	good	world-famous author	none

(continued)

FAMILY UNIT D	3 people, two female and one male, together (not married) for four years					
	male	40	college graduate	115	good	bank president	none
	female	40	high school dropout	125	good	homemaker	none
	female	39	Masters Degree in Business Administration	115	good	owns clothing boutique	none
FAMILY UNIT E	2 people, one male and one female, together (not married) for five years					
	male	38	Ph.D. in biology	135	good	homemaker	none
	female	36	college graduate	140	good	world-famous photographer	travels on assignment a great deal

A view of a public park, 1970's, before population control was instituted.

communication actions

running a simulation-game

In "Population Control 2204" each role is taken by, or given to, a different person—or, if possible, group of persons. Note that there are five family units, some with two and some with three members; there can be an unlimited number of witnesses for each family unit. The idea is to try to involve as many people as possible. For ease of identification, each person writes his or her role-title on a name tag (blanks available p. 143) and pins it on. Next, the Situation Statement is read aloud by the teacher or a student, and the action is started by all members of each separate family group and its witness(es), if any, and the Population Control Board Member(s) getting together in separate groups to read the rest of the "Population Control 2204" materials and to plan what they will say at the open session of interviews called by the Population Control Board Member(s). To help communication during the simulation-game, each person can use a Simulation-Game Work Sheet at the back of the book. Next, everyone is called together by the Population Control Board Member(s) for the open interview session where the participants informally act out what they think would go on at such a meeting. Finally, the role-group responsible for making a decision confers and announces its ruling.

sharpening skills

In addition to running a simulation-game by informally acting out "Population Control 2204," you can use the materials in the simulation-game as a basis for sharpening your skills in the four areas related to effective communication in English: speaking, listening, reading, and writing.

SPEAKING ACTIONS

1. Suppose that you are a child born on Permit #1 to one of the five family units (you choose which) in "Population Control 2204." Assume that it is twenty years later, and you have been asked to come before your local neighborhood Population Control Board to tell them if they made the correct decision in selecting your family unit. Develop the speech you would give. As you do so, remember that your audience will want to hear the reasons behind your opinion.

2. Suppose that you are living in the year 2204 and you want to apply for one of the Population Growth Permits available in "Population Control 2204." Select the specific permit you would want, and then develop the speech you would give when applying to the Population Control Board. As you do so, remember to present the advantages you would offer as a parent for the permit you chose.

3. Suppose that the Population Control Board in the year 2204 is considering the creation of your clone—an exact carbon copy of you. Assume that you have been asked to appear before the Population Control Board to speak either in favor or against the creation of your clone. Develop the speech you would give.

4. Take a position on the issue of birth control at the present time. Assume that you have been given a chance to air your views on a local television community-affairs program. Develop the speech you would give. As you do so, remember that the audience will need you to explain the reasons behind birth control before you give and support your opinion about it.

5. Be prepared to defend or oppose any one of the following debate topics:
   (a) The population bomb threatens to create an explosion as dangerous as the explosion of the H bomb.
   (b) Marriage as we know it today is outdated.
   (c) "No woman can call herself free until she can choose consciously whether she will or will not be a mother." (Margaret Sanger)
   (d) "A baby is an inestimable blessing and bother." (Mark Twain)

LISTENING ACTIONS

1. Ask someone who is adopted—or someone who has adopted— what are some of the advantages and, if any, disadvantages of adoption. (If you do not know anyone who is, or has, adopted, ask people you know to assume that they were adopted or that they might adopt a child.) Listen to the responses, for the opinions and underlying attitudes toward children and family life.

2. Ask a physician, clergyman, or teacher what he or she thinks it takes to be good parents in today's world. Compare what you hear with the concerns for good parenthood expressed by the Population Control Board Member in "Population Control 2204."

3. Take a poll among 15–20 people by asking them if they think that the growth of the world's population should be controlled. As you listen to the answers, try to hear not only the specific answers but also the underlying attitudes about the future. As you take your poll, take brief notes and then see if you can discern patterns in the answers.

4. Listen to expectant parents as they speak about having a baby. What are their feelings? What are their worries, if any? Is there any difference between what the woman and the man says? Is there a difference in what is said if it is to be a first baby or if there are already children in the family? Is any mention made of the characteristics that the parents hope their child will have? Try to hear underlying attitudes the people have about themselves and children as well as the specific content of their answers.

Reread "Population Control 2204," following the SQ3R (Survey, *Question, Read, Review, Recite*) approach discussed in the Reading section in the chapter on communication skills at the back of this book. The SQ3R approach will make it easier for you to become familiar with all the material in "Population Control 2204."

*Detailed Reading
and Reacting*

Here are questions that will call upon your ability to read for main idea, major details, inferences (getting at underlying attitudes), and then to form your own opinions. Sharp skills in these four reading areas will help you to be an expert reader.

I.   *Main Idea*

   A.   What decisions does the Population Control Board of local neighborhood TN3 have to make?

   B.   From reading the "Important Communication" and the "Population Control Manual: Definitions Section," what do you think is the general idea of population control in A.D. 2204?

II.   *Major Details*

   A.   The Situation Statement

      1.   How many permits are available and how many family units are competing for them?

      2.   Why did the planet reorganize itself over 150 years before A.D. 2204?

   B.   The "Important Communication"
      What are the major characteristics of each growth permit?

   C.   The "Population Growth Manual: Definitions Section"
      What is the Cloning process and the Decompression Therapy process?

   D.   The Photographs
      What does each photograph show?

   E.   The Roles
      What intangible factors about each family unit are of interest to the Population Control Board Member?

III.   *Inference*

   A.   The Situation Statement
      Why are the applicants required to plea in person before the Population Control Board?

   B.   The "Population Control Manual: Definitions Section"
      Why does the opening statement to the manual say, "planning of quality is as important as planning of quantity"?

   C.   The Photographs
      What is the effect of the showing of the second and the last photographs along with the scientific photographs?

D. The Roles
What is implied by these items about the family units: if married, distribution of sexes in the unit, age, educational background, I.Q., health, occupation, and special comments?

IV. Opinion

A. What do you think of the population control arrangements of A.D. 2204? Explain.

B. How would you allot the three Population Growth Permits among the five family units? Why?

Vocabulary Study   Here are some words you have read in "Population Control 2204." (They are listed in the order in which they appeared.) Do you know the meaning of each? For a discussion of how to study vocabulary, look at the Reading section of the chapter on communication skills at the back of this book.

contraception	decompression therapy
compulsory	abdomen
ineligible	pelvis
decreed	atmospheric pressure
conception	fetus
artificial insemination	abstract thinking
prenatal	random
cloning . . . cloned . . . clone	test-tube breeding
impregnated . . . impregnation	fertilized
uterus	intangible
ovulation	emotional stability
sperm cells	compassion
descendant	

Additional Reading

1. Look under "genetics" in the card catalog of your college or public library. See if there are any books about human genetic engineering, and compare the information you find with that given in "Population Control 2204."

2. Look under "marriage" in the card catalog of your college or public library. If there are any books about new marriage styles, read them and compare what you read with the family unit types given in "Population Control 2204."

3. Be on the alert for newspaper articles and editorials about genetic engineering or about new marriage styles. What is the attitude of the writer toward each of these futuristic issues?

WRITING	As a result of taking part in the simulation-game "Population Control
ACTIONS	

**WRITING
ACTIONS**

As a result of taking part in the simulation-game "Population Control 2204" (or just reading it), you can probably think of many ideas to write about. Below are some suggestions for both paragraph and essay topics. The topics range from those directly related to "Population Control 2204" to those on the general topic of population control, genetics, and marriage. For your convenience, any topic that fits into one or more of the rhetorical forms mentioned in the Writing section of the chapter on communication skills at the back of this book is followed by one or more of these symbols in parentheses: D for description; N for narration; Def. for definition; P for process; R for report; and A&P for argument and persuasion.

Paragraph Writing

1. Select any one Population Control Permit in "Population Control 2204" and decide which family unit you would give it to. Write a paragraph in which you present and explain the reasons for your choice. (A&P)

2. Would you like to be the parent of a super-intelligent child? Write a paragraph in which you state and explain your answer. (A&P)

3. What are your best characteristics? Your worst? Write a paragraph in which you explain which of your characteristics you would like your children to have. (D)

4. Should sterilization (an operation that prevents reproduction but not sex) be forced by the government on people who are considered by some "undesirable"? (This was done, for example, in the United States in the early 1970's to two young women who were supported by welfare funds.) Write a paragraph in which you present and support your views about forced sterilization. (A&P)

Essay Writing

1. How would you distribute the Population Growth Permits in "Population Control 2204"? Write an essay of recommendations in which you discuss each permit and the reasons for your awarding it to one of the family units. Assume that your essay will be read by the Population Control Board that is responsible for the final decisions. You might also want to include a report on the open interview session, as well as your evaluation of the suitability for parenthood of each of the five family units. (A&P, R, Def.)

2. Is there someone you particularly admire? If so, would you like to be his or her clone? (See the "Definitions" section of the "Population Control Manual" in "Population Control 2204.") Write a narrative essay in which you are the clone of someone you admire. Tell what your life is like and how it feels to be who you are. (N)

3. Looking back on your childhood and thinking about your own parents and the parents of your friends, can you formulate your definition of a good parent? Write an essay in which you develop your definition. As you do so, try to draw heavily on specific examples from your experience. (Def., N)

4. Do you think people should bring children into today's world? Write an essay in which you present and support your answer. As you do so, remember that your opinion will be shaped both by your feelings about children and your feelings about the modern world. (A&P)

5. What would the world of the future be like if characteristics in newborn babies were controlled? Would such genetic engineering improve the world? Write an essay in which you argue for or against genetic engineering. As you do so, try to think of the effect of genetic engineering on individuals as well as the world-at-large. Also, try to describe your vision of the future. (A&P, P)

6. Read through the speaking, listening, and opinion reading questions given for "Population Control 2204." Write an essay on any one of the topics that interests you.

7. Do you want to get married someday? (Or if you are married, would you get married if you could do it over again?) Today there is much discussion about the advantages and disadvantages —both for a woman and for a man—of getting married. Write an essay in which you discuss the reasons for, or against, getting married. (A&P)

8. Would you like to be part of a group marriage rather than a marriage of just two people? Or, do you think a marriage contract should be for five-year periods, renewable upon the consent of both parties? What other alternatives to traditional marriage forms can you think of? Write an essay in which you discuss and evaluate alternative marriage styles. As you do so, remember to consider the impact of your ideas on the individuals in the marriage-form, the children of that marriage, and society as a whole. (A&P, Def.)

9. Here are some statements about birth control, population control, the family, and the future. Select one statement that interests you and develop an essay around it: (A&P, Def., P)
   (a) "Prevention of birth is precipitation of murder." (Tertullian)
   (b) "The hungry world cannot be fed until and unless the growth of its resources and the growth of its population come into balance." (Lyndon B. Johnson)
   (c) "The family is one of nature's masterpieces." (George Santayana)
   (d) "I like dreams of the future better than history of the past." (Patrick Henry)

COMMUNICATION SKILLS:

a resource chapter

writing

Well, here I go again. Face-to-face with another writing assignment. I'd rather talk than write anytime. It all comes out okay that way. But when I write . . .

Don't panic. Writing is not a great mystery—indeed, for some people it's a happy challenge, demanding at times but rewarding when the finished product is ready. Giving advice on how to write is as easy as dispensing aspirin: Many millions of words have been written about writing.

But the advice has to work for you. Perhaps you'll find, for example, that it will help you to separate out pieces of that seemingly enormous thing called "writing." To start with, you might find it useful to know that there are three somewhat different kinds of writing: description, narration, and exposition. Often they overlap, but for the sake of clarity, let's look at each kind separately.

DESCRIPTION

What does a penny look like? "Silly question," you might say. But it isn't as silly as it might seem. Even something as small and simple as a penny can be described with spirit and imagination. All it takes is a close look beyond its obvious charcteristics to its effects on all of the five senses (sight, touch, hearing, smell, and taste) and to its various uses. Whether you want to give the reader a mental image of something small or something as large and complex as a city, before you can describe it, you have to observe it carefully. Then select the specific details that will give the reader an accurate impression of what you see, hear, feel, smell, and taste. Notice how sense images are used to create a strong impression of the Dry Gulch College cafeteria:

The Dry Gulch College cafeteria is a disaster area. With dirty gray walls and a dull black tile floor, the cafeteria looks like a well-lit cave. The serving area, which is just to the right of the entrance, is dominated by a long metal counter that ends at a clanging cash register. Behind the counter, — **sound**

sight wafer-thin hamburgers and spicy frankfurters sizzle on a — **smell and taste**
greasy grill while the fishy odor of tuna salad sandwiches — **smell**
fills the air. Crowded into the remainder of the cafeteria, dozens of wooden tables and uncomfortably hard chairs — **touch**
are hidden beneath candy wrappers, empty milk cartons, and the other leftovers of hastily eaten lunches. About the only necessity missing from the cafeteria is an ambulance entrance for use by those who fall victim to the vile food

100 *communication skills*   and unhealthy atmosphere.

The writer's message is clear: The cafeteria should be condemned by the Board of Health. As you can see, a good description uses all the senses to create a lasting, dominant impression.

NARRATION

Almost everybody likes to read a story. Whether it's a comedy or a mystery, people are curious to know what is happening. In most narrations events go on in a specific setting and time sequence. Notice how the following excerpt from a narrative immediately establishes the time and the story's physical background or setting:

As he headed down the crowded corridor to his

10 A.M. math class, Roy spotted Linda Roberts, one of   *setting*

time

the most attractive and popular girls at the college. Deciding

that this would be a good opportunity to get to know her,

he strolled over to Linda and started a conversation about a

mutual friend of theirs. Linda smiled warmly and participated

freely in the discussion that lasted more than fifteen

minutes. Encouraged by her receptive manner, Roy finally

asked her for a date. "Where would you take me?" Linda

asked sweetly. Roy's jaw dropped as he pictured the single

five-dollar bill that had to last the rest of the week. "How

about going to McDonald's for a hamburger?" he suggested.

With a stunned look on her face, Linda snapped, "How

about getting lost?" And she turned quickly and walked

off down the hall.

When you write narration, you also have to decide who is telling the story. The narrative above uses the third-person point of view: That is, someone other than the people in the story explains the events and even tells what Roy is thinking. If either Roy or Linda were telling the story, the slant of the story, the point of view would probably change drastically.

EXPOSITION

What do a report about a five-car accident, a recipe for banana-fudge dip, and an article about acupuncture have in common? All give you information, and that's what exposition is about—the giving of information. In addition, exposition often includes some supporting elements of narration and description. The report of the car accident, for example, would probably contain a narration of how the accident occurred and a description of what the smacked-up cars looked like.

But in the report the purely expository facts would be given primary emphasis.

Because exposition is the type of writing you'll be doing for most of your college courses, let's take a closer look at what goes into writing an expository essay:

Getting Started

What are you going to write about? That's always the first step— you have to choose a subject. So, if at all possible, select a subject that you are interested in so that your writing will reflect your enthusiasm. But watch out: Make sure that your subject isn't too broad for an essay. For example, if your subject is college, you could easily write a full-length book about it. So, for an essay, you have to limit your area by dividing it into sub-areas:

COLLEGE

courses	faculty
grading	students
sports	facilities
clubs	rules

Which one appeals to you the most? You can choose any of the items on this list, but even then you still have to do some more narrowing-down and limiting. For instance, if you select "students" as your area, you could limit it further to a discussion of the pressures on students or the students' involvement in school government. If you don't know enough about your topic to limit it properly, try looking through the index of a book on the subject. The index will list many areas of a subject, any one of which you might like to explore further.

Okay, now let's assume you've found your specific writing area: the pressures on college students. Next, you need to ask yourself: What about my topic? For example:

Question: What *about* the pressures on college students?
  Answer: The pressures on college students are more of a burden than most people realize.

The answer would be the thesis statement, or main point, of your essay. The thesis statement establishes your purpose in writing the essay and controls the type of evidence you will use to develop your point of view.

Gathering Information

Can you back up your point of view? If not, your essay won't "work." So, after you've worked out a thesis statement that states your point of view, it's time to gather evidence to support it. Happily, your first source of information is yourself. Your everyday experiences and the knowledge you've picked up from books, movies, television, and newspapers have turned you into a vast storehouse of information on many subjects. But sometimes you may discover that you don't have enough information on hand. In that case, research will be necessary. Perhaps you can start your research by talking with people who will provide you with additional facts and points of view about your subject. Then it's a good idea to go to the library to consult relevant books and periodicals. When you do so, you should usually rewrite in your own words any information you get from publications. However, if the information is especially well phrased, you may want to use it exactly as it appears in the publication. Just be sure to use quotation marks to indicate that the wording is not your own.

Organizing the General Expository Essay

Thinking ahead isn't always very popular, but it pays off when you are writing exposition. So, once you've collected your evidence, it's best to work out an essay plan. If you do this, you'll be able to get your material across with more success. Here's one possibility for an essay plan:

GENERAL EXPOSITORY ESSAY PLAN

Introductory Paragraph: Capture readers' interest and present your thesis statement.

Body Paragraph One: Give first subordinate idea and supporting evidence.

Body Paragraph Two: Give second subordinate idea and supporting evidence.

Body Paragraph Three: Give third subordinate idea and supporting evidence.

Concluding Paragraph: Briefly restate central thesis; if appropriate, make a plea for action or change in attitude; end with a memorable send-off.

Suppose you wanted to follow this plan when writing about the pressures on a college student:

Body Paragraph One: the pressure of keeping up with school work
Body Paragraph Two: the pressure of paying school expenses
Body Paragraph Three: the pressure of having a satisfying social life

Although this plan is for a five-paragraph essay, it could easily be expanded to a longer paper by adding additional subordinate ideas. There's one thing to be especially careful of: Don't let your subordinate ideas overlap. For example, if you added a fourth subordinate idea on the pressure of taking tests, you would probably end up repeating some of what you wrote in your paragraph on keeping up with school work.

If you have trouble thinking of three subordinate ideas for an essay, you might try using one of these idea patterns for an expository essay:

SOME COMMON EXPOSITORY ESSAY IDEA PATTERNS

A. Past	A. Personality	A. Science
B. Present	B. Character	B. Business
C. Future	C. Ability	C. the Arts
A. Home	A. Childhood	A. the Individual
B. Business	B. Adulthood	B. the Community
C. Leisure Time	C. Old Age	C. the Nation

These patterns aren't rigid, so feel free to use part of a pattern together with a few of your own ideas or with part of another pattern. Just make sure that your parts fit together into a logical whole.

In addition to these general expository essay idea patterns, here are other patterns to help you organize a report, a definition essay, a process essay, and an argument and persuasion essay.

Organizing the Report Essay

What happened? That's not an unusual question. And sometimes you may be expected to answer it by playing the role of a crackerjack reporter. You might be called on to report on such events as a meeting of the karate club, a car accident in the school parking lot, or a biology experiment with a skunk. Whatever you're supposed to report on, your first decision is whether you are going to write a subjective or an objective report. A subjective report gives the details as well as your personal reactions to them, and an objective report gives only the facts, allowing the readers to form their own reactions. Here's an essay plan for either type of report:

REPORT ESSAY PLAN

Introductory Paragraph:	Tell what event you're reporting on.
Body Paragraphs:	Give full details in the order they happened. (The number of body paragraphs will depend on the length of the event and the number of details you include.)
Concluding Paragraph:	Tell how the event ended. If a subjective report, give your personal reactions to the event.

As you can see from this plan, in a report your details should be arranged in chronological order, the order in which the event occurred. And as you go along, be sure that you give all the important details so that the reader will be able to picture exactly what happened.

Organizing the Definition Essay

"Look it up in the dictionary" is popular advice. But how can someone write a full essay about a definition? By going far beyond a brief dictionary definition, a well-planned definition essay explains what something is. Such an extended definition stimulates thought and provides a fresh approach to a topic. For example, if you're defining love, you might go beyond the male-female relationship to discuss the love of a child for his pet or the love of a dictator for his power. The following plan can help you pull the elements of your definition essay into a unified whole:

DEFINITION ESSAY PLAN

Introductory Paragraph:	Tell what is being defined and explain what's worthwhile about defining it.
Body Paragraph One:	Deal with one aspect or part of what you're defining.
Body Paragraph Two:	Deal with a second aspect or part.
Body Paragraph Three:	Deal with a third aspect or part.
Concluding Paragraph:	Draw conclusions about what is being defined.

Using this pattern, you could define a concrete subject such as an automobile by discussing its exterior appearance, its interior appearance, and its motor. Or you could define an abstract idea such as fear by discussing fear of embarrassment, fear of the dark, and fear of the supernatural.

Organizing the Process Essay

Would you like a chance to be a teacher for a while? As a student, you've been learning for so long you would probably welcome the chance to do some teaching. The process essay gives you that opportunity. You might teach the reader how to make pizza, or how the rotary engine works, or how you lost fifty pounds on a well-known weight watching diet. Whatever your topic, in a process essay you give the steps in the process in chronological order, that is, the order in which they happened. Your total essay plan, however, will vary according to the type of process you are explaining:

PROCESS ESSAY PLANS

For the *How to . . . Essay*:

Introductory Paragraph:	Tell what the process is and explain why it's important to know.
Body Paragraph One:	State the materials or qualities needed for the process.
Body Paragraph Two:	Give the steps in the process. (If there are many steps, additional body paragraphs will be needed.)
Concluding Paragraph:	Describe the result of the process and praise or criticize it.

For the *How . . . Was Done Essay* or the *How . . . Works Essay*:

Introductory Paragraph:	Tell what the process is and explain why it's important.
Body Paragraphs:	Give the steps in the process in chronological order. (The number of body paragraphs will vary according to the number of steps.)
Concluding Paragraph:	Challenge the reader to think and explore further.

To keep the process from being a dry list of facts, tease the reader's curiosity with appropriate incidents or surprising facts. For example, if you are explaining how to make homemade wine, you might mention that the consumption of wine in the United States has doubled in just the last three years.

Organizing the Argument and Persuasion Essay

Most likely you have some strong opinions bottled up inside you that you're simply dying to let out. The argument essay is your chance. But the argument essay is not merely a vehicle for blowing off steam. If you want to persuade others to agree with your opinions, you'll have to back them up with facts and specific evidence. Personal judgments and emotional reactions alone are not very convincing. To see the clear difference between a fact and a judgment, compare the following:

Fact:	More than 57 percent of American households have at least one pet.
Judgment:	Pets make wonderful companions for small children.

A fact, then, is an objective statement that can be confirmed by measurement, observation, or research. Solid facts are the ammunition that you need to win your argument. A good essay plan also helps:

ARGUMENT ESSAY PLAN

Introductory Paragraph:	State the issue being discussed and give your opinion.
Body Paragraph One:	Give a reason for your opinion and back it up with supporting evidence.
Body Paragraph Two:	Give a second reason for your opinion and back it up with supporting evidence.
Body Paragraph Three:	Give a third reason for your opinion and back it up with supporting evidence.
Concluding Paragraph:	Reemphasize your opinion and urge its adoption.

A special type of argument essay is the "position paper." Position papers are written by many types of people, including politicians, executives, and community workers. Position papers present background facts and information as well as state the writer's position or opinion on the subject. Often the purpose of a position paper is to recommend something or to urge the reader to action. This type of argument essay combines persuasion with elements of description and reporting. You'll find this essay plan for a position paper especially useful for reacting to some of the simulation-games in this book.

POSITION PAPER ESSAY PLAN

Introductory Paragraph:	State the purpose of the conference and tell who attended it.
Body Paragraph One:	Describe the problem.
Body Paragraph Two:	Offer a solution.
Body Paragraph Three:	Attack opposing views.
Concluding Paragraph:	Make a call for action.

These argument essay plans will be more effective if you support your opinions with dramatic incidents as well as definitions of key terms. Above all, your evidence should be strong enough to prove your case; you shouldn't simply insist that you are right without telling why.

PARAGRAPHS After you've worked out your essay plan, you'll be ready to start writing your paper. Here are some pointers to help you build effective paragraphs.

The Introductory Paragraph Don't take anything for granted. Although the title of your essay may reveal your subject, be sure to state it clearly in your introductory paragraph. Your thesis statement is useful for this. In addition, you should use your introductory paragraph as bait to catch the reader's interest. You might employ any of several devices as an attention-getter. For example, here's an incident used as a teaser to lure the reader into an essay entitled: **The Pressures on a College Student.**

incident

After flopping down into her seat, Helen straightened up and tried to listen attentively to Professor Marino's history lecture. But Helen's mind soon began to wander, her body relaxed completely, and her eyelids slowly closed. She dozed quietly for half an hour until she was suddenly awakened by a hand vigorously shaking her shoulder. When she realized that the hand belonged to Professor Marino, Helen's face instantly reddened with embarrassment. "Didn't you get enough sleep last night?" Professor Marino asked coldly and immediately walked away without waiting for an answer. Indeed, Helen had not gotten any sleep the night before because she was working as a waitress at a local

essay topic

diner to pay for her school expenses. This need to earn money is just one of several pressures that Helen—and a great many other college students—face today.

You may also get attention with a startling fact, a provocative question, or an appropriate quotation. Whichever device you choose, avoid expressions such as: "Now I will tell you about . . . ," "I would like to discuss . . . ," or "In my paper I will explain. . . ." These expressions, and others like them, are too obvious and self-conscious.

The Body Paragraph The body paragraphs form the heart of your essay, because in these paragraphs you sell your ideas to the reader. To put across your ideas successfully, you need to develop each paragraph with a bit of structure and a good deal of convincing evidence.

The structure is provided by a topic sentence that introduces the paragraph. This topic sentence tells the reader what the paragraph is about. Play it safe and put your topic sentence at the beginning of your paragraph, for it can sometimes be wrong to put the topic sentence in the middle or at the end. Also be sure that your topic sentence is limited enough to be developed effectively in one paragraph. For example, compare these two topic sentences:

Too Broad: A college education is very important in today's world.
Well Limited: A college education is an important requirement for most good jobs.

The "too broad" topic sentence above would force you to discuss all of the advantages of a college education in just one paragraph. The result would undoubtedly be very shallow and unconvincing. On the other hand, the "well limited" topic sentence above would allow you to discuss one advantage in some detail.

After writing your topic sentence, you then have to back it up with specific evidence. The following paragraph will give you an idea of the types of details you might use:

One of the greatest pressures on students is the need to keep up with their college professors' course requirements. At Freshman Orientation, the extent of these

name

requirements was made clear by President Drought when he

name

said, "Doing homework is an opportunity for you to expand

quote

your mind; at Dry Gulch you will have many such opportunities." He was not exaggerating. Last Thursday, for example, Professor Ravine assigned one hundred pages of

name   *number*

War and Peace for Monday and Professor Tangent

name   *name*

announced she was giving a math test the same day—

which, unfortunately, was also the day my twenty-page

history paper was due. To get this done, I read

War and Peace all Friday night, studied math all day

name

Saturday, and worked on the paper from 8 o'clock Sunday

incident   *number*

morning until 3 A.M. Monday. I managed to deliver the

number

paper just after my professor had dismissed the class and

was walking out the door. I computed that I had spent

thirty-eight hours of the weekend working on my assign-

number

ments, which was equivalent to the amount of time I

spent on all the work I did in high school. It's a wonder

that only 50 percent of the freshman class drops out.

number

Notice how the details—the numbers, names, quotation, and incident—all support the topic sentence. A sentence about a student's financial pressures or about Dry Gulch College's extracurricular activities would have interfered with the paragraph's purpose and the argument would have been weakened. So make sure that all of your details directly support your topic sentence.

In addition, be sure that you use enough details. How many details are enough? That all depends on your topic. If you are explaining the principles of karate, you would probably need fewer details than if you were advocating the legalization of marijuana. The more controversial topics require more details to persuade the skeptical reader.

The Concluding Paragraph

The last is often the best remembered. So send your reader away with a bang. As you do so, remember that the concluding paragraph should flow naturally out of the body of the essay. Your ending should tie up the package and give it a feeling of completeness. When possible, drive home the major point of your essay, leaving the reader with a strong impression of what you've said. You might use any of several methods for this purpose. For example, a recommendation for specific actions is the basis for the following conclusion to an essay entitled: **The Pressures on a College Student.**

a call for action
> Students must learn to budget their time and money carefully. They should try to keep up with their homework assignments so that they don't accumulate too much to do at the last minute. In addition, students should seek the advice of a school counselor who is trained to help with educational and financial problems. And what will the result be? Control. For when students meet pressures head on, half the battle is won.

Another method of concluding an essay is to restate the major points—using new words—to help the reader remember what was said. Or you might reemphasize your thesis statement by using a quotation, a question or an incident. Whichever method you use, be sure to avoid absolute statements such as: "This proves that . . ." or "If we take this action, the problem will be solved." No matter how strong your evidence, you can never prove or solve something completely. So try to be more accurate by qualifying these statements: "This seems to prove that . . ." or "If we take this action, we will be helping to solve the problem."

COHERENCE
Your ideas might be great, but if they don't all hang together in a unified whole, you will probably just confuse the reader. The use of topic sentences, supporting details, and introductory and concluding paragraphs will help you to create a unified external structure for your essay. Internal unity can be achieved with the use of pronouns, key words, and transitional words and expressions. These devices link together the sentences in the following section of an essay entitled: **The Ingredients of a Long Life.**

Living in a placid environment that minimizes stress,

these people have an average life expectancy of 84 years.

Such evidence indicates that a lack of tension can add

valuable years to a person's life.

In addition, many scientists believe that a vegetable

diet is an important factor for longevity. To prove their

theory, they point to societies with an unusually large

number of very old people. For example, in the Caucasus

Mountain range in Southern Russia, over 5,000 people are

more than 100 years old, with the oldest believed to be

almost 170. Scientists attribute this to a diet comprised

mostly of vegetables, particularly lettuce, cabbage, beans,

spinach, corn, celery, and parsley. Also cited as areas of

longevity are Vilacamba in the Ecuadorian Andes, South

America, and the Hunza Region of Pakistan. In these two

areas, fresh vegetables are even more important, with

meat and dairy products constituting only 1.5 percent

of the total diet.

Although the vegetable diet's effectiveness in

prolonging life has yet to be scientifically proven,

it is a known fact that daily exercise is a key ingredient

for a long life. Various kinds of exercises

Left margin labels: transition, key word, pronoun, key word, key word, key word, key word, key word, kev word, key words

Right margin labels: key words, pronoun, transition, key word, key word, transition, pronoun

Pronouns   Notice how pronouns are used to link the first two sentences of the full
                          paragraph in the selection above.

> Furthermore, many <u>scientists</u> believe that a vegetable
> diet is an important factor for longevity. To prove <u>their</u>
> theory, <u>they</u> point to societies with . . .

This is a simple method of maintaining coherence. But be careful: Be
sure that your pronouns clearly refer to a specific word.

Key Words   Ideas can be connected by the deliberate repetition of certain key
                          words. For example, in the selection above, the words *vegetable, diet,
                          old,* and *longevity* are repeated because they are central to the con-
                          tents of the paragraph. You'll find that key words are useful for linking
                          sentences. But use key words like a good spice in food, sparingly for
                          effect, not heavily for boredom.

Transitions   What's the connection? To make it clear and avoid a choppy writing
                          style, you can use transitional words and expressions. Such transitions
                          create a bridge between sentences and show a relationship between
                          ideas.

> Choppy: The birthplaces of the Presidents of the United States
>   include houses, apartments, and even motel rooms. No
>   American President was ever born in a hospital.
> Smoother: The birthplaces of the Presidents of the United States
>   include houses, apartments, and even motel rooms. *How-
>   ever,* no American President was ever born in a hospital.

Opposite this page are five groups of the more popular transitions.
When you use them, be careful to select the most appropriate transition for the sentences you want to bridge. Also, don't sink your paragraphs with the weight of too many transitions: Three or four in a
150 word paragraph are plenty.

As you've probably figured out by now, writing is a system, not a
mystery. So the next time you're faced with a blank page to fill, make
it easier for yourself by following these steps: First select your subject
and formulate a thesis statement. Then work out an appropriate essay
plan and develop each paragraph with topic sentences and specific
details in your body paragraphs. Don't forget to use pronouns, key
words, and transitional words and expressions to pull all of the pieces
together. Finally, it's also a good idea to use a dictionary to check your
spelling and an English handbook to check your grammar and punc-
tuation.

Writing is a good way to get your message across, so make the most
of it!

ADDITION WORDS in addition furthermore moreover also equally important	To avoid buying fewer unnecessary items in a supermarket, eat a full meal before you go shopping. *In addition,* stick closely to a grocery list that you have prepared beforehand.
EXAMPLE WORDS for example for instance thus in other words as an illustration	Lightbulbs come in a variety of sizes. *For example,* the smallest lightbulb is hardly bigger than a grain of rice while the largest is about the size of a bass drum.
RESULT WORDS as a result consequently therefore thus hence accordingly	Dolphins are highly intelligent sea creatures known for their friendly, relaxed temperament. *As a result,* they are being trained to aid frogmen in naval intelligence work.
CONTRAST WORDS in contrast however but nevertheless on the other hand on the contrary at the same time	A motorcycle can go up to ninety miles on a gallon of gasoline. *However,* riding a motorcycle is four times as dangerous as driving a car.
TIME WORDS yesterday then soon next today first tomorrow second immediately meanwhile finally at last	To study for a test, *first* read through your notes completely, picking out the major points to be studied. *Then* recopy any important names and dates to imprint them in your mind. *Finally,* read your textbooks to fill in any gaps in your notes and to reinforce what you have already studied.

reading

Have you ever had such thoughts? Most people have, especially when they have to read something they're not particularly interested in. Feelings of being overwhelmed by reading come in large part from a rigid idea of what reading is. So let's get one thing straight. Everything is *not* read the same way. It all depends on what you're reading. Some material has to be read slowly and carefully while other material needs only a quick once-over.

Reading your textbook and other non-fiction books calls for the slow, careful approach. But here's something that will make it easier:

THE SQ3R APPROACH

SQ3R is not the secret code name of a special potion that when swallowed gives instant knowledge. But SQ3R is the formula devised by reading teachers to help people read factual, informative material. SQ3R stands for

> **S** u r v e y
> **Q** u e s t i o n
> **R** e a d
> **R** e v i e w
> **R** e c i t e

SQ3R tells you that there's more to reading than starting with the first word and continuing to the last word. It's hard to wade through pages and pages of words if you nail yourself to every word, one after the other. SQ3R tells you, therefore, that before you start reading each word, you need to get an overview of the material. Only then should you start to read. Even when you do read, though, SQ3R tells you that you can use your judgment to combine skimming with careful, slow reading. SQ3R also tells you that once you've reached the last word, it's best not to stop until you've made yourself a summary of what you've just read. Luckily, though, when you use the SQ3R approach, your summary is partly done even before it's started, because your summary starts with the overview gained from the Survey and Question parts of SQ3R and goes on from there.

Using SQ3R, you can approach reading the same way you might approach a painting. When you look at a painting, you don't start at the upper left-hand corner, look across the top part of the painting, return your eyes to the middle left edge, go across the middle, and so on. Rather, when you look at a painting, you first look at its overall subject, then at its main features, and next at its details. Finally, when you turn away from the picture, you can describe it to someone who has not seen it.

As you use the SQ3R approach, follow the lead of the letters S Q R R R on the chart on the opposite page.

HOW SQ3R WORKS

S	Survey	This is a previewing skill. It means look over everything *before* you read the first word of the first paragraph. Do this: • Look at the beginning and the end of the entire material —how long is it? • Look at the title—what does it mean? (If you are not sure, keep asking as you continue to Survey.) • Look at the subtitles and subheadings—can you begin to see the plan of the material emerging? • Look at the pictures and graphs as well as their captions —what information do they give? • Rapidly read any introductory, concluding, and summary paragraphs—do they tie in with your impressions of the material gained from your other Survey techniques?
Q	Question	This is another previewing skill. It means turn each title and heading into a question. (For example, for the title "Women on Patrol" ask: What kind of patrol? What kind of women?) Often, the answers to your questions give you a good grasp of what the material is all about.
R	Read	As you read through the material, keep in mind the overview you have from your Survey and Questioning, and do this: • Read key paragraphs and sections carefully. • Skim less important paragraphs. • Note vocabulary words you are not sure of and plan to study them later. • Adjust and enlarge your overview as you come to important new details.
R	Review	This is a recall skill. It means try to remember what each main section said *as it relates to the overview*. Feel free to select the important and put aside the less important, but don't forget information that matters.
R	Recite	This is another recall skill. It means take the information you have and tell someone else about it. You can do this by: • Speaking about it by answering questions, making an oral report, or participating in a discussion about it. • Writing about it by outlining, taking a written test, or writing an essay.

That's what the SQ3R approach is all about. And as you work with it, you'll find that various reading tools will come in handy. Some of them are vocabulary study, graph and illustration reading, and outlining.

VOCABULARY STUDY

Learning new words is something everyone wants to do, but only some people actually do. There's just one way to do it: get started. As you read, you might begin by simply underlining words you don't know. The chances are that you'll begin to notice that some of the same words keep reappearing over and over again. It's those frequently used words that need your attention most of all.

Try putting each word you want to learn on one side of a 3 × 5 inch index card and the word's meaning on the other. As you're riding the bus or taking a walk, whip out the cards and go through them by looking at the sides containing only the words. If you can't remember a meaning, turn the card over and read it through. After you do this a few times, meanings will begin to stick.

The payoff comes when you're reading and can remember the meaning of a word you've just studied. It won't always happen, but as you study words more, you'll find it happening more often. Watch out, now. Just because you don't remember a meaning, that doesn't mean you don't remember *anything*. The first step to a good memory is becoming aware of *what* exactly you want to remember. So, recognizing that you "almost" know something is halfway home!

If you have an "idea" of what a word means but you aren't sure, try figuring it out from the context—that is, from the word's placement in the sentence and from the other words around it. Of course, if you have no idea of what a word means, you'll have to look it up. But be selective. Concentrate on words that are basic to what you are reading. No one can master all unknown words at once, so it's best to start with the crucial ones.

By the way, how about the word *crucial* in the last sentence? Could you figure it out from the context? If not, look it up, and get it onto a 3 × 5 inch card because it's a crucial word to know.

Another crucial reading tool is graph and illustration reading.

GRAPH AND ILLUSTRATION READING

"One picture is worth more than ten thousand words" is an old Chinese proverb that certainly applies to graphs and illustrations. When you come across them in factual, informative material, you can be pretty sure that they say something not easily said in words alone. Although graphs and illustrations are visuals, they have to be "read" just as words are.

Read a photograph? Yes. Keeping your overview of the reading material in mind, look at the subject and the mood of the photograph, and tie it into the whole package. If there's a caption under or over the photograph, your job is even easier, but whatever you do, don't ignore those pictures. They'll be a big help.

SAMPLE PIE GRAPH

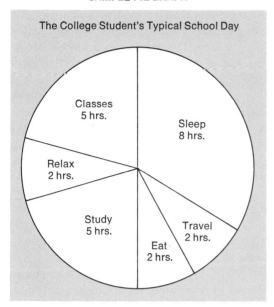

The College Student's Typical School Day

Classes 5 hrs.
Sleep 8 hrs.
Relax 2 hrs.
Study 5 hrs.
Eat 2 hrs.
Travel 2 hrs.

SAMPLE LINE GRAPH

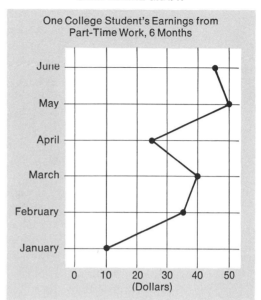

One College Student's Earnings from Part-Time Work, 6 Months

June
May
April
March
February
January

0   10   20   30   40   50
(Dollars)

SAMPLE PICTOGRAPH

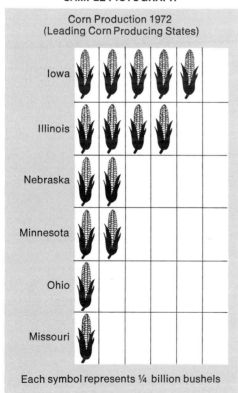

Corn Production 1972
(Leading Corn Producing States)

Iowa
Illinois
Nebraska
Minnesota
Ohio
Missouri

Each symbol represents ¼ billion bushels

SAMPLE BAR GRAPH

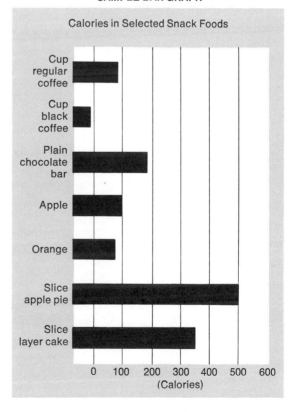

Calories in Selected Snack Foods

Cup regular coffee
Cup black coffee
Plain chocolate bar
Apple
Orange
Slice apple pie
Slice layer cake

0   100   200   300   400   500   600
(Calories)

So will cartoons. But cartoons aren't always funny. Some are dead serious as they poke fun at something. If a cartoon doesn't strike you as amusing or even understandable right away, don't give up. After looking at its characters and reading the caption and any labels in the cartoon, go through the rest of the material you're reading and then come back to the cartoon. Chances are that its meaning will eventually become clear to you, and when that happens, you'll be rewarded with seeing an extra dimension in what you're reading.

Graphs and charts are tricky, but they can't be ignored. They might look complicated at first glance, but they're a great help for getting a capsule view of exactly what is going on. Usually, charts summarize while graphs summarize and show relationships. Reading a graph is something like decoding a puzzle, so look at it piece by piece. Don't let yourself ignore anything on display: the title, the labels, the layout. Perhaps a look at the four most frequently used types of graphs will help you become comfortable with: the pie graph, the bar graph, the pictograph, and the line graph.

Seem like a lot to absorb? Well, don't be discouraged. Once you've learned how these four types of graphs work, you'll be able to handle most of the graphs you'll run across in your reading. True, each new graph you read will be displaying different information, but most formats are one of the four shown: pie, bar, line, and picture.

The advantage of illustrations is their usefulness in summaries. Another useful summary reading tool is outlining.

OUTLINING

When you look at the outline below, don't read it *all* immediately. Skim it, moving your eyes so that they focus first on only the most important items. What's most important? The title and the main ideas (marked with Roman numerals: I, II, III) are.

Problems at Dry Gulch College
  I.   The Cafeteria
       A.   Tasteless food
       B.   Overcrowded
  II. The Library
       A.   Noisy
       B.   Not enough books
            1.   More copies of heavily used books
            2.   More new titles
  III. The Student Lounge
       A.   Not enough chairs
       B.   Not enough lockers

Now that you know which problems get star billing at Dry Gulch College, read the subordinate ideas (marked with letters: A, B) to find out the major details of each main type of problem. Finally, read the minor details (marked with numbers: 1, 2). You probably now have a fairly clear summary picture of Dry Gulch's problems. As a result, if someone asks you what's happening at Dry Gulch, you would be able to give a thumbnail sketch, stressing the main ideas and filling in the details as needed.

Now let's go the other way. How do you make an outline from what you are reading? First, pick out the main ideas—and make sure they're really *main*. Some ideas have to be subordinate. Part of developing skill in reading is being able to decide what's important and what's not so important. Very often in factual, informative material, the headings and subheadings provide you with your main ideas, which you then outline with Roman numerals. You can often get your major subordinate details by finding key sentences in paragraphs. (Label subordinate ideas in an outline with capital letters.) Depending on how much material you are outlining, you can also include minor details that will help you recall the information you want to hold on to. (Label minor details in an outline with Arabic numbers.)

Although much of your reading can be handled with the SQ3R approach, some material demands that you read closely for information and then react personally to what you have read.

DETAILED READING AND REACTING

Well, what do *you* think? This question is usually not stated in your reading. But when the material has to do with controversial issues, your personal reaction to what you've read is expected to be part of the reading package.

It's easy to let your emotions run away with you, so be careful and go slowly. First, you have to get all of the basic information that the material is trying to give you. Only later can you have the luxury of letting loose with your own opinions. Detailed reading and reacting consists of four basic steps, each designed to lead you closer to informed, intelligent reasoning and reacting. The chart on the next page shows you how detailed reading and reacting works.

HOW *DETAILED READING AND REACTING* WORKS

Main Idea	Use SQ3R to get a general idea of what the material is about.
	• If it's a paragraph, look for the central thought of the paragraph—most of the time it's the first, last, or middle sentence.
	• If it's a section or a short chapter, look at the various headings and subheadings—and then read the material as it relates to those headings.
	The idea is to get the general, broad contents of the material.
Major Details	Fill in the major subordinate details to give a fuller picture to the main ideas.
Inferences	Take what you've read a step further, and try to "read between the lines." What underlying attitudes are reflected in what you've read?
	• Has the author tried to sway you with "loaded language" that feeds on common prejudices?
	• Has the author made clear distinctions between what is fact and what is opinion?
	• Has the author referred to experts by name or are the references based on heresay?
	The idea is to be critical as you read so that you can figure out what is implied as well as what is stated.
Opinions	It's your turn. But don't rush it. Be sure you have a command of the information given you (main ideas and major details) and the implications behind the information (inferences). Now, what do *you* think?

Detailed reading and reacting can be quite an interesting challenge. A textbook on human physiology or electronic engineering might not necessarily engage the reader in developing his or her personal opinions. But a great deal of reading invites you, the reader, to join in—to reason, to argue, and, perhaps, to take action. Newspaper editorials, books and essays, and magazine articles that present a point of view are designed to stimulate your personal involvement—just as simulation-games do.

speaking

What is this guy talking about anyway? Did he just say something about collecting butterflies? I thought he was supposed to be speaking about the French Revolution. What was that about sex scandals? Or did he say six candles? The way he mumbles he could be cursing everybody in the room and we wouldn't know it. Oh, well, who cares? I can always use a little more sleep.

Sound familiar? You have probably had a similar mental conversation when you had to listen to a speaker who just rambled on in a low voice without stating his thoughts clearly. "How could he do this to me?" you wondered as your eyelids slowly closed.

Of course, the speaker did not deliberately want to bore and confuse you. He just didn't know the basic principles of good speech-making. Whether it's a group discussion or a formal speech, there will be times when you are called on to address a group of people. To communicate with them effectively—and to avoid putting them to sleep—try to follow these guidelines:

SPEAK UP!

Your ideas may be the best since Einstein's Theory of Relativity, but if you don't speak loudly enough, your brilliance will remain a well-kept secret. To help overcome the jitters, take a deep breath before speaking to relax your vocal cords. Keep your chin up and imagine that you are talking to the person farthest from you. That way you are sure to be heard. But try not to sound as if you are reciting Greek tragedy; if you pretend that you are talking to just one person, you will maintain a conversational tone that listeners appreciate. It's also a good idea to regulate the quality of your voice to avoid speaking in a boring monotone. By raising and lowering your voice level, you can indicate a question, stress important words, and make contrasts clear.

In the same way, you should vary the pace of your speaking. If you talk too fast, your listeners will quickly be buried in an avalanche of ideas. So try to maintain a speed of about 125 words a minute. To get a feeling of the proper pace, read aloud the following paragraph in thirty seconds:

> Many television advertisements lure us with misleading statements. "For the strength of Atlas, eat Cruncho Cereal!" one commercial shouts, while another promises, "Drink Diet Delight Soda to develop the slender, youthful figure of a dancer." And "For the soft skin of a baby, wash with Sudsy Soap." Thus, for a dollar's worth of assorted products, you can chop ten years from your age. Truly amazing!

How long did it take you? If you read the paragraph aloud in less than thirty seconds, you need to slow down. Try to speak in thought units, pausing between thoughts to let the listener absorb your words. Don't forget to pronounce each word carefully so that the listener can understand. Finally, you can stress major points by pausing dramatically and emphasize a few key words by saying them very slowly.

STRAIGHTEN UP!

Let's face it. Just about everyone is nervous when he or she has to deliver a speech. But you can hide your shakiness by maintaining good posture. To appear more confident, you should stand up straight with your weight evenly distributed on both feet. At the same time, avoid the stiff wooden-soldier look that will make your audience know you feel uncomfortable. While occasional forward body movements will effectively emphasize a point, constant pacing back and forth might make your audience a little seasick. If you keep your hands in a relaxed position at your sides and use natural gestures from time to time, you will give the appearance of someone who knows what he is talking about.

During a discussion you are generally sitting when you speak, but good posture is still important. If you are slumped over with your elbows resting on a table, you will look lazy and indifferent. If you rest your head in your hand, you will look tired and bored. Instead, you can project your voice better by sitting slightly forward on your chair with your hands either in your lap or resting on the edge of your desk or table.

SMILE!

Nothing will turn off a listener faster than a speaker with a deadpan expression on his or her face. So smile and show enthusiasm for your subject. When you do, you make the listener feel relaxed and receptive to your ideas. (And you even strengthen your facial muscles.)

As you speak, slowly move your eyes over the audience, pausing occasionally to look directly at specific faces. In this way, you will make each person feel that you are talking to him or her, and that's just what you want. You will lose this valuable rapport if your eyes are glued to your notes or if you fix your eyes on only one person.

Speak up, straighten up, and smile—whether you are taking part in a discussion or delivering a speech, these are important guidelines to follow. Now here are some additional pointers for specific speaking situations:

WHEN PARTICIPATING IN A GROUP DISCUSSION

If a group discussion is to be worthwhile, you can't just talk off the top of your head. Before coming to the meeting, you should formulate your opinions and gather facts to back them up. You may even want to use 3 × 5 inch index cards to record your information, especially statistics and quotations.

Even if the group discussion is spontaneous, as sometimes happens in your classes, you will be a more effective participant if you think before you speak. Before you talk, formulate the general point you want to make, and you will sound more confident and avoid rambling on without a clear goal. In return, your listeners will get a strong impression of your ideas.

When it is your turn to speak, get to your ideas quickly to avoid boring the other participants and monopolizing the discussion. Also, if the topic under discussion calls for defending or opposing a point of view, your opinions should be labeled clearly with expressions such as "It seems to me . . ." and "In my opinion . . . ." After giving your own point of view, you might attack the opposing positions, but do it tactfully. Instead of saying "You're wrong and here's why," you would have a better chance of winning over the opposition with "Your ideas are interesting but I have some doubts because . . . ." By maintaining the "yes, but" attitude, you show respect for the other person's view and the open-mindedness needed to reach a fair conclusion.

WHEN PREPARING A FORMAL SPEECH

You may know a hilarious joke about an octopus, but don't tell it in the middle of your speech on prison reform. If you do, you will weaken your argument and confuse your audience. To avoid getting sidetracked, an effective speaker organizes his presentation so that it has a beginning, a middle, and an end:

GUIDE FOR A FORMAL SPEECH

  I. Introduction:
     Capture listeners' interest and state central thesis
  II. Body of Speech:
     A. Give first subordinate idea and supporting evidence.
     B. Give second subordinate idea and supporting evidence.
     C. Give third subordinate idea and supporting evidence.
  III. Conclusion:
     Briefly restate main and subordinate ideas; if appropriate, make a plea for action or change in attitude; end with a memorable send-off.

As you plan your speech, you should keep in mind the type of audience you will be addressing. If the people are not experts on your topic, you will want to include basic information and define any unusual terms they might not know. If the audience is going to be composed mainly of one particular age or occupational group, you will want to emphasize what is most interesting to that group.

Introduction

If the members of the audience are not automatically interested in your speaking topic, they may just tune you out. But you can grab their attention by using your introduction as bait. You might begin with an anecdote, a quotation, a striking fact, or a provocative question. Naturally, whichever device you use, it should be relevant to your topic. Another effective method is to stress the importance of your subject by explaining why it is of current interest and by indicating how it may influence the listeners' lives. For example, if you are speaking to a group of students about the dangers of drug addiction, you can point out that in the past year over 2,000 Americans died from drug abuse and that about 200 of these people were teenagers. With this information, you are indirectly telling the students that they should be interested in your topic because people like themselves are involved.

In addition to catching the listeners' interest, a good introduction includes the central thesis of the speech. To avoid sounding wishy-washy, the central thesis statement should indicate a strong point of view regarding the topic. "I am going to talk about drug addiction" is weak in comparison to a strong statement such as "Drug addiction can destroy a person physically, mentally, and socially."

Body of Speech

After luring the audience with your introduction, you then want to present convincing evidence in the body of your speech. You do this by first dividing your central thesis into subordinate ideas that support your point of view. For instance, if your topic is the need for women's liberation, you might speak about discrimination against women in the home, in the business world, and in social activities. The number of subordinate ideas that you discuss will depend on the amount of time allotted for your speech. It's better to develop a few ideas fully than to skim over several ideas superficially. It's best, if at all possible, to have more than one subordinate idea.

To support each of your subordinate ideas convincingly, you might use a variety of evidence: statistics, quotations, incidents, examples, and comparisons. For example, suppose that you are speaking about the need for women's liberation and your first subordinate idea is that women are discriminated against in the business world. This subordinate idea could be supported with many types of evidence:

EXAMPLE OF SUPPORTING EVIDENCE

A. First Subordinate Idea: Women are discriminated against in the business world.

   Supporting Evidence: 1. Describe an incident in which a highly competent female bookkeeper was passed over for promotion because her boss thought of her as "just another dumb blond."

   2. Give statistics comparing the salaries earned by men with those earned by women. Also give statistics comparing the numbers of men and women in executive positions.

   3. Give several examples of job opportunities and salaries, indicating how they differ according to the worker's sex.

   4. Quote an official of the Department of Labor who knows of research to prove that women are discriminated against in the business world.

To get your evidence to stick together as a unified whole, you should use transitions. Words and expressions such as "however," "therefore," "in addition," and "for example" will help you to link sentences and paragraphs so that your speech will flow smoothly. (See list of transitions on page 113.) In addition, certain transitional words are useful for emphasizing the subordinate ideas in your speech. For example, if you say that you are going to discuss three points, you might label these points: first, second, third.

Conclusion   The conclusion is your last opportunity to drive home your point of view. You can do this most effectively by restating your central thesis and subordinate ideas and by telling the listeners what they should do, believe, or understand as a result of your presentation. To tie the whole speech together, you might also refer to something you said in the introduction. For example, if you used a quotation to open your speech, you can conclude by indicating how your major ideas support the quotation.

PRACTICE YOUR SPEECH!

Only a professional actor or actress can make a memorized speech sound spontaneous, and nothing is more boring to an audience than a singsong recitation. So instead of memorizing your speech, you should rely on notes to guide you. First, write out your speech and read it several times to familiarize yourself with the material. Then pick out the key phrases, statistics, and quotations and print them by hand on index cards. Be sure that the print is large enough to see two to three feet away, which is often the distance between your eyes and the surface you rest your notes on as you speak. Using the cards, you should practice in front of a mirror to check your facial expressions, posture, and gestures. You might even tape-record your presentation to evaluate your timing, clarity of speech, and vocal variety.

listening

Bob: I missed Professor Poltergeist's lecture last night. How was it?

Andy: Great! He talked about the supernatural. You know, ghosts and stuff like that.

Bob: What did he say about them?

Andy: Gee, I don't remember. But he told this wild story about an old lady from Boston. Or was it an old man from Portland? Well, it was something like that.

Bob: Are you sure you got anything out of it?

Andy: Yeah, it was very informative.

Informative? Well, Professor Poltergeist's lecture probably was, but Andy obviously didn't listen to it very carefully.

Half-listening is not unusual. We all do it at times. Who could be blamed for not paying much attention to a dog food commercial or a television interview with a rock star high on drugs? On the other hand, many situations do deserve more careful listening. If you have a job, you need to listen to your boss and fellow workers, or you may soon find yourself unemployed. And if you're going to school, you'll find that lectures, class discussions, and informal talk among students will all draw upon your ability to listen.

Unfortunately, people are not born with good listening habits. The ability to be a good listener is an acquired skill that must be learned and then practiced. So the next time that you are in a situation that requires careful listening, try applying these basic principles:

AVOID DISTRACTIONS

A Rolling Stones record playing on the radio . . . two friends sharing the latest gossip . . . a newspaper headline announcing "Five Naked College Students Arrested"—such sights and sounds are all around you to lure your attention. But as a skillful listener, you tune out distractions and even avoid the temptation to whisper to someone next to you. Instead, it's best to look directly at the speaker, showing interest in what he or she is saying. Although it's not polite to interrupt while someone is still talking, you can react with slight changes in your facial expressions and body position. When you respond this way, you'll find the speaker will welcome these signs that you are interested.

And since the speaker's ideas are what you are after, you'll also want to ignore his or her mannerisms, appearance, and unusual speech qualities. If you are distracted by, let's say, a speaker's nervous habit of head scratching or finger tapping, you know you're going to miss much of what is being said. Similarly, don't let yourself reject a speaker just because his clothes are wrinkled and shabby or because he has the misfortune to resemble a werewolf. Above all, try not to be influenced or bothered by the quality of someone's voice. Don't assume that a person with a high, squeaky voice has nothing important to say. A person who speaks with a Brooklyn accent or who makes mistakes in grammar is not necessarily stupid.

CONCENTRATE

"Hang in there" is good advice for effective listening, for concentration is probably the greatest necessity for a good listener. But if you maintain the attitude that listening is really participating mentally in a conversation, your ability to concentrate will be much improved. Did you know that people can absorb a speaker's words faster than he or she can say them? This means you have some extra time when you're listening. So don't waste it by daydreaming about your latest date or your plans for the weekend. Instead, make yourself use the time to summarize mentally the speaker's thoughts. When listening to a lecture or formal speech, you'll find it easier to pick out the important points if you remember that an effective speaker deals with one main idea that is supported with subordinate ideas that, in turn, are supported with many facts and examples. As you listen to the speaker's anecdotes, statistics, and quotations, be sure to keep in mind the ideas they are supporting. After all, it's the ideas that you want to grasp.

So pay special attention to the speaker's opening, for it's here that he is likely to state his main topic and indicate that he plans to discuss five major points or to suggest three possible solutions. Then, as he develops his ideas, try to listen for certain transitional words and expressions that are clues to the importance of what the speaker is about to say. The subordinate ideas may be clearly indicated with words like "first," "second," "third," and "finally." The supporting facts and examples may be introduced with "for example" and "for instance," while "in summary" and "in conclusion" might be used to signal the ending. The ending is especially important because the speaker will usually restate his main points, giving you the opportunity to pick up any key ideas you may have missed.

As you mentally collect each idea, rephrase it briefly in your own words to make sure that you really understand it and to imprint it in your memory. If a point is not clear, make a mental note to ask the speaker to clarify, explain, or repeat it.

BE OPEN-MINDED BUT CRITICAL

Suppose that Senator Blowhard angers you by suggesting that all students should have their heads shaved. If you immediately turn him off, you will not discover that he might have some great ideas for new legislation to improve job opportunities for college graduates. So you can see that, as you listen to a speaker, it's a good idea to remain open-minded even though you may disagree strongly with some of the ideas you hear. You can make a fair evaluation of a speaker's ideas only after you've heard all that he or she has to say.

At the same time, you must be critical of what you hear. Is the evidence logical and accurate? Or is it vague and exaggerated? If the speaker claims that tests prove that cigarette smoking is not harmful to your health, ask yourself *what* tests? If he uses statistics supplied by the Puffo Tobacco Company, ask yourself if there is reason to be suspicious of this evidence. If he quotes a baseball player who endorses cigarette smoking, ask yourself if the quote comes from an authority on the subject.

Just as a speaker may try to persuade you with misleading evidence, he or she may also use a more subtle method—loaded language. Loaded words are charged with an emotional content that can make you instantly angry or happy. Advertisements for cosmetics lure customers with such positive words as "youthful," "clean," and "glamorous." A politician, on the other hand, might try to manipulate your feelings with "Communism" and "enslavement," words that would probably make you react negatively to a person or idea. This is a trap, so evaluate everything you hear as you search for solid evidence.

It's also important to "listen between the lines" to pick up any underlying attitudes that the speaker may have. For example, if your friends call you a "big spender," do they sincerely mean it? If there is a touch of sarcasm in the way they say "big spender," they might really be calling you a tightwad. Similarly, if a man says that he lets his wife out occasionally, he is unintentionally revealing that he thinks of himself as his wife's keeper.

TAKE NOTES

Did you know that after two weeks people forget more than 75 percent of what they hear unless they make a special effort to remember? Taking notes helps. When you listen to a lecture or speech, taking notes keeps you on your toes and tells the speaker that you consider his remarks worth recording. More importantly, your notes will provide you with a handy reference that will supplement your memory.

There's a danger, however: Note-taking is a definite aid, but don't get carried away with it. Even if you can write with the speed of a stenographer, don't take too many notes. If you do, you will probably miss the enjoyment of the speech and end up with a tired wrist. As you listen to a speaker, jot down just the major points he is making and any questions and comments that you may want to offer when the speaker is finished. Use arrows and underlinings to set off especially significant information. Then read over your notes promptly, making sure that you understand everything that you have written. If the speaker rambled on without organizing his thoughts carefully, your notes will probably be somewhat confusing and you will have to rewrite them in a logical order. But it's time well spent, because you will end up with a useful source of information as well as a better understanding of the subject.

simulation-game
support materials

SIMULATION-GAME WORK SHEET

Your Role: _____ _____

In the Simulation-Game called: _____

_____

SPEAKING: What will your role-group say at the meeting?

_____

LISTENING: What are the opposing positions to your role-group?

131   continued on other side

LISTENING: What decisions were made at the meeting?

SIMULATION-GAME WORK SHEET

Your Role:_____ _____

In the Simulation-Game called:_____

_____

SPEAKING: What will your role-group say at the meeting?

_____

LISTENING: What are the opposing positions to your role-group?

133   continued on other side

LISTENING: What decisions were made at the meeting?

SIMULATION-GAME WORK SHEET

Your Role:

In the Simulation-Game called:

SPEAKING: What will your role-group say at the meeting?

LISTENING: What are the opposing positions to your role-group?

135

continued on other side

LISTENING: What decisions were made at the meeting?

SIMULATION-GAME WORK SHEET

Your Role:_____ _____

In the Simulation-Game called:_____

SPEAKING: What will your role-group say at the meeting?

LISTENING: What are the opposing positions to your role-group?

137

continued on other side

LISTENING: What decisions were made at the meeting?

SIMULATION-GAME WORK SHEET

Your Role: _____

In the Simulation-Game called: _____

_____

SPEAKING: What will your role-group say at the meeting?

_____

LISTENING: What are the opposing positions to your role-group?

continued on other side

LISTENING: What decisions were made at the meeting?

SIMULATION-GAME WORK SHEET

Your Role: _____

In the Simulation-Game called: _____

_____

SPEAKING: What will your role-group say at the meeting?

_____

LISTENING: What are the opposing positions to your role-group?

141   continued on other side

LISTENING: What decisions were made at the meeting?

SIMULATION-GAME NAME TAGS

(One per person per game.)

index

EXTENSION GAMING SERVICE
University of Michigan Extension Service
412 Maynard Street
Ann Arbor, Michigan 48104